AF374640

Dedication:

To my wife – thanks for all the sacrifices

To my kids – thanks for all the joy

To Snoop – thanks for all the encouragement

Special thanks to Mr. Richard Belcastro for his help and support, especially with the front and back cover design.

Table of Contents

Introduction

I hope two things: that you enjoy teaching and that your teaching leads to student learning. That's it in a nutshell. People say to "start with your why". Before I get to that, let me share what I've heard lately - teachers are stressed, tired, feeling underappreciated, and overall dissatisfied. Smart, hard-working, committed teachers are walking away. It's a shame and, more than that, it's a potential crisis. So, here's "my why" for writing this book - I don't want any more teachers to walk away. I don't want to continue to hear about teacher burnout. I don't want to see adults who dedicated years studying and thousands of dollars to earn a teaching degree, decide after a few years that it's not what they had hoped for. I don't want to see adults who start out with the best intentions to work with children and help shape their lives decide that it's not for them anymore. Here's what I do hope - I want you to wake up excited, teach a full day and leave school invigorated. I want you to educate students, but I also want you to challenge, motivate, and inspire them to become the best they can be. I want you to feel great every day. I don't ever want you to feel overwhelmed, defeated, or discouraged to the point of giving up — EVER! There may be challenges, but never something that you cannot overcome. I've worked in education for over 25 years, and I've taken a lot of mental notes. Typically, the school year goes something like this: teachers are rested and excited for a new year, after a few days the excitement remains, and the entire staff is saying, *"This year seems better than last"*. Within a few weeks, however, the stress is building. Among other things, there are emails to respond to, a new curriculum to learn, meetings to attend, and a new district initiative on social and emotional support for students. After a month, the papers for grading have piled up and deadlines are looming. After two months parent-teacher conferences are approaching, and grades are due. In addition to the everyday tasks of instruction, the teacher has agreed to coach a sport and sponsor a club and is now feeling the "weight of the world" on his or her shoulders. By Halloween (if not sooner), the teacher is frazzled and is going home exhausted. The rest of the year is spent trying to maintain some semblance of balance and play catch up. By the end of the year the teacher has decided to either a.) stick it out at the school hoping next year will be better b.) leave for another school in hopes that "the grass is greener" elsewhere or c.) get out of teaching altogether. I don't want this to be your experience. **I want your first day to be productive and enjoyable, but I want your last day, and every**

<u>**day in between, to be the same.**</u> So that's "my why". A lot of this book gets into the "what" and the "how", but please know that my intention is never my way or the highway. My suggestions for how to have an enjoyable and productive year are simply that – my suggestions. If those suggestions resonate with you and you see value incorporating them into your process, great! If, after reading my suggestions, you think of ways to tweak something to make it your own, please do. You must own whatever it is you decide to do, and not do it simply because I suggested it. I'm excited to share my thoughts with you through this book, but ultimately please know that each of you can make your experience unique to you. There are certain non-negotiables (like you'll read right away in chapter one), but you can and should incorporate your finishing touch to everything you decide to do. The last thing before we get rolling is this: it's darn

near impossible to write a book that EVERY K-12 teacher can benefit from. I worked on an elementary campus for five years and one of the challenges was to provide professional development to the range of teachers from kindergarten to 8th grade. It's not impossible, but there are inherent challenges. So, most of this book can apply to most grades and most teaching situations, but there may be things for you to consider adjusting depending on your situation. So, are you ready? Remember, I want your first day to be enjoyable and productive, but I also want your last day and every day in between to be the same. Sound impossible? I'm here to tell you it's NOT. So, let's begin.

Chapter 1 – Setting the tone

Teachers have a variety of personalities and what works for one teacher may not work for you. The good news is that you don't need to be someone that you are not. You can be yourself for the entire year, but here is the nonnegotiable: **You MUST put certain expectations and procedures in place starting from the first second your students step foot into your room**. Notice how I wrote "MUST". Expectations and procedures are not optional. You must have them to set the tone for the entire school year and to increase the chance of having a more enjoyable, more productive experience. Remember, I want you to go home every day invigorated.

Expectations and procedures

Before the students arrive for the first day, each student's full name should be written on an index card that is taped to the desk (taped so it remains in place). If you have multiple periods with different students, then the index card should have a period number and the student's full name. (See Illustration one).

Period 1 – John Silva

Period 2 – Margarita Sotelo

Period 3 – Sally McPherson

Period 4 – (Prep period)

Period 5 – Jim Watson

Period 6 – Dante Smith

(Illustration one)

The following should be written on the whiteboard at the front of the room:

Mr./Mrs./Ms. <u>(Teacher's last name)</u>

Welcome to <u>(name of class)</u>

Please find your name on an index card and have a seat

Please begin filling out the student survey that is

on your desk

As students walk into your classroom on day one, greet them at the door. Smile and be friendly, but not overly friendly. Greetings such as, "welcome", "nice to see you", and "glad to have you in my class" are friendly and professional. Greetings such as, "Hey girl, I like your shoes" or "Nice shirt, my man" are unprofessional and should be avoided. From the first moment your students meet you, they should see you as an adult and as a professional. In addition to a professional and friendly greeting, instruct entering students to "please read the board and follow the instructions on it". You want your students to establish the habit of reading the instructions on the board, hearing your instructions once, and then being able to do what you have instructed them to do. This is the system you will use throughout the year, so you are starting day one by training them in that system.

Q: What's the why for saying instructions AND writing them on the board?

A: It makes the instructions clear to students and minimizes the time and energy you will spend giving them.

Let's fast forward into the school year a bit and consider two scenarios in which two different teachers give instructions to their class. The first teacher does NOT write the instructions on the board, but the second teacher does.

<u>Scenario one</u>: **Teacher does NOT write instructions on the board**

Teacher: "OK, guys quiet down, quiet down (some students continue talking). You guys need to read pages 46 and 47 and compare and contrast the structure of DNA and RNA. You guys got that? Any questions? (Still some talking among students) Ok, go ahead and start."

Students: Some begin working, but most hesitate because they are unsure of what to do. Some are still talking to a classmate. Finally, one says to no one in particular "What page?"

Teacher: "Guys, guys, c'mon get quiet. I said pages 46 and 47. C'mon, you two get your stuff out. Start reading."

Students: A few more are working, but many remain talkative or unsure of the assignment.

Teacher: "C'mon guys. Let's go. Hey, you guys, I'm going to count to three. One, two, let's go!"

Christine: (a straight A student that wants to get her work done): "Mrs. Davis. What do we do? Are we listing what makes up each molecule?"

Teacher: "No, don't just make two lists. You should compare and contrast."

Ben: (a student that is trying harder each week): "What's compare and contrast?"

Teacher: "We've talked about that already in this class. Compare is to find similarities and contrast is to find differences."

Dylen: (a student from the back of the room): "Differences for what?"

Teacher: (Frustrated and raising voice) "DNA and RNA - Hey, Let's go you guys!"

Piper: (a student from the other side of the room): "Miss... what page again?"

Teacher: (Exasperated) "C'mon!"

This scenario might sound silly or exaggerated, but I promise you it is not. I've seen this type of interaction far too often. Many teachers become demoralized as students drain them of their energy by making a simple task (like reading two pages) a challenge. That's why throughout the year you should put a system in place to eliminate any ambiguity your students may have while preserving the time and energy you have. **The way you'll do this is by writing instructions on the board and saying them once**. Now let's consider scenario number two in which the teacher always writes instructions on the board.

<u>Scenario two</u>: Teacher always writes instructions on the board

Teacher: "Class, eyes and ears on me in three, two, one." (The teacher waits and observes to make certain that all students have put their pen or pencil down, have turned to face the teacher, and are quietly attentive ready to listen to instructions). "Excellent. Thank you for your prompt attention. It is appreciated. At this point, it is my hope that you all have a clear understanding of the structure of DNA and RNA. Please refer to the instructions on the board as I explain my expectations. (Teacher stands by the board and points to the first instruction). For the next 15 minutes, you will work individually and read pages 46 and 47 silently. (Teacher points to next instruction). After you read, please create a Venn diagram* comparing and contrasting the two molecules. We have compared and contrasted earlier this year using a Venn diagram, but as a reminder, to compare means to find similarities and to contrast means to find differences. (Teacher points to the last instruction). I would like you to list at least three examples in each section of the Venn diagram."

*(Later in the book I'll show how to effectively use a Venn diagram).

Teacher continues: "With your shoulder partner**, I would like person one to explain to person two what my expectations are."

*(**Later in the book I'll explain how to create a shoulder partner for each student by numbering the students "one" or "two").*

The teacher takes a lap around the room as the "ones" explain to the "twos" what the expectations are. The teacher ends up back in the front of the room after approximately 30 seconds.

Teacher: "Eyes and ears on me in three, two, one. Excellent, I heard some outstanding explanations. I would like everyone to be prepared to share with the class what my expectations are. Please do not raise your hands. I want everyone to think about it and be prepared to answer. (Provide a wait time of five seconds before calling on a student). Gianna, would you please explain the expectations to the entire group? You may refer to the instructions on the board if you need to."

Gianna: "We are going to read pages 46 and 47 individually and silently. We are then going to create a Venn diagram in which we compare and contrast the molecules DNA and RNA."

Teacher: "Fantastic, thank you Gianna. Class I want you all to be prepared to answer this question, how many should you list in each section of the Venn diagram? (Wait time of five seconds). Diego?"

Diego: "We should list at least three in each section".

Teacher: "Excellent. Thank you, Diego. Class, are there any questions?"

(A student, Rafael, raises his hand). "Class, please be respectful and attentive to Rafael. Rafael?"

Rafael: "In the center of the Venn diagram where the circles overlap, we should write the similarities, correct?"

Teacher: "Yes, exactly Rafael. Thank you for double checking. Are there any other questions? (The room is quiet). Great, you may begin, and I am setting the timer for 15 minutes."

Which scenario seems like the one you would like to experience? I am 100 % confident that you would prefer scenario number two. Notice how the teacher only gave the instructions verbally one time. Additionally, the instructions were written on the board for students to refer to throughout that entire lesson. This seemingly simple method of writing the directions on the board and verbally giving them to students once is simple and effective for you and ***it is what's best for our students.*** If students rely on us over and over for simple things (like listening and following directions), we are robbing them of the opportunity to develop life skills such as respectfully listening, following directions, and asking appropriate clarifying questions. Those skills will help them long after being students in our class, so it is important to help them develop them starting from day one in your classroom.

 Let's go back to the first scenario in which the teacher becomes exasperated explaining the instructions to her class. I have seen countless times when a teacher has _that_ experience and _then_ spends the next 15 minutes walking around as students raise their hands and inquire "What do we do?". The teacher, already frustrated and tired, spends the majority of the 15 minutes re-explaining the directions to individual students that have learned to be helpless. Let's contrast that scenario with scenario two in which EVERY student knows what to do and has begun in a quiet and productive setting. The teacher now has fifteen minutes to use how she chooses. Maybe she goes to her desk and enters the quiz grades from the day before, or responds briefly to an email, or thinks ahead to the next part of the lesson and prepares the room, or signs certificates of accomplishment that she had printed for the students that earned an A on the last quiz, or signs certificates of improvement for the students that made improvement from assessment one to assessment two, or types the next vocabulary list for the following week or just sits quietly so as to be available for students that seek help, or slowly walks the room checking on students and providing feedback as they work towards the objective. The point is that the teacher that can create a classroom environment and culture like scenario two can choose how to spend his or her time and energy as students work productively. You can do this starting from the first minute of day one. ___Say it once and write it on the board___ for students to read. Create a culture in which students are expected to engage and be attentive. Encourage and appreciate them when they do. Finally, use your time and energy the way you want when students are working in your classroom.

Now, let's get back to the first minute your students walk into your classroom on day one. You continue to greet students in a friendly and professional manner. Students are finding their seats and beginning the survey that you placed on their desks. Your instructions are written on the board because you are training them to listen to you one time and read the board to confirm what you have instructed. Congratulations! You have set the tone for the entire year in the first few minutes, but we are only getting started so let's continue, shall we?

Chapter 2 – The first few minutes and the "micro-conversation"

You greeted students with a "Welcome, nice to see you" and now most of your students have arrived. Your instructions are written on the board at the front of the room to train students to look for them throughout the year. At this point all students that have arrived have found their name on an index card, have sat down, and have begun working on the student survey that you left on every table (*more on the student survey in a minute*). At this point, the room may be completely silent. The fact is, you WANT the room to be silent as each student begins to fill out his or her survey. It may seem a bit awkward at first. There are probably between 25-35 new students, and you might not know any of their names. This may be your first time seeing your students and you may be a stranger to them. The natural tendency of most teachers is to break the silence or try to do or say something fun or funny. A teacher may choose to start the year by talking about who he is, why he became a teacher and all the exciting things he wants students to learn. This typically goes on for 10 minutes and then there is some sort of icebreaker designed to allow students to get to know each other. Students would mill about the room with a handout that might include prompts such as the following:

Find someone that...

1. owns a dog

    ____

2. has the same number of siblings

    ____

3. plays a sport

    ____

The handout might contain ten (or more) prompts for students to match with a classmate and write down his or her name. This would go on for about 20 minutes, at which time students would return to their seats. After this, the teacher would discuss the syllabus until it was time for the students to dismiss. I want to STRONGLY discourage starting the school year this way. As the school year progresses, there will be time for the students to get to know you (within professional boundaries of course) and each other. Creating a positive classroom environment is a critical part of every school year but allowing the students to get up and walk about on the first day is counterproductive. First, it sends a message to students that your class is fun and games. Second, it relinquishes most if not all your authority in the first ten minutes. Students do better when they know who is in charge so set the boundaries and save the fun and games for the end of the year party.

So, what should you do? Let's talk about that, but first let's talk about the survey that students are busy filling out.

Q: What is the why for giving students a survey?

A: A survey allows students to share who they are with you, it gives students something productive to do immediately upon entering your classroom, and it allows you to get to know your students which will help build a positive and productive culture in your classroom.

The survey contains ten "get to know you" prompts that each student will answer individually and silently. Some sample prompts might include:

1.) My perfect Saturday would be...

2.) If I could eat dinner with anyone it would be...

3.) If I could do anything for a living I would...

4.) The person I most respect is...

5.) The extra-curricular activities I want to be involved with this year are...

After the last prompt, create a more open-ended prompt such as: "**Write anything else that you think I should know (for example – do you...like to sit near the front, speak another language, have pets at home, have brothers and sisters, etc.).**"

I like to include this final prompt because it allows students to tell me some interesting, pertinent things that they may not have told me in any of the other prompts. For example, some students might write that they work two jobs to help pay bills or that their main language is Spanish or that they live with their grandmother or that they prefer to sit near the front or that they own two German Shepherds or that they like basketball or any other piece of information that they are comfortable sharing and feel is important. Again, my suggestion is ten prompts plus the last open-ended section but remember to leave enough space in between each to allow students to write a clear and complete response.

Overall, the purpose of the survey is threefold:

1.) Students get a chance to write about themselves (which they typically enjoy).

2.) You get a chance to get to know your students which will allow you to have "micro-conversations" with them throughout the year (more on "micro-conversations" in a moment).

3.) It keeps students focused and productive from the first second they walk into your classroom and find their seat.

All three of these reasons are important, however #3 is especially important. Walking in your classroom and getting started on a survey sends a message to your students that they are expected to be productive and work from the first second that they enter your class. I can't think of a better way to start the first minute of the first day of class.

After about 10 minutes, students should be finished, and you will collect their surveys (more on collecting papers in the next chapter). Once collected, you can put the surveys aside, but it is important that you take the surveys and study them like you were studying for your hardest final exam. The reason is simple, but absolutely one of the most critical things you will do throughout the school year — "the micro-conversation". What is a "micro-conversation" you ask? As you know, micro means small in Latin, so a "micro conversation" is a conversation between you and a student (or a handful of students) that usually lasts a small (short) amount of time - usually between 10 – 45 seconds. Here are two examples of potential "micro-conversations" that could occur during the school year.

<u>**Two examples of a "micro-conversation" that could occur as students enter your class:**</u>

After taking the surveys home you read your students' responses about their "perfect Saturday" and discover that one student (let's call her Sarah) would take her two German shepherds to the dog park. You also read that your new student Jacob would go to the gym and play basketball on his perfect Saturday. The next day, you recall this information to engage in a "micro-conversation", first with Sarah and then with Jacob:

Teacher: "Good morning, good to see you."

Students: "Good morning."

Teacher: "Good morning, Sarah. What are your German Shepherds' names?"

Sarah: (A bit surprised, but happy to share) "Brownie and Baxter."

Teacher: "Nice. I had a German Shepard as a kid. They are great dogs, huh?"

Sarah: "Yes, they are! I love my Brownie and Baxter!" (As she walks through the door and finds her seat).

Teacher: "I bet you do. Good morning, guys. Good morning, everyone."

Students: "Good morning."

Teacher: "Hey Jacob. You like basketball. Who's your favorite team?"

Jacob: (Also a bit surprised, but happy to share) "I'm a Bulls fan."

Teacher: "Bulls? Booooo, I'm a Celtics fan. Hey, are you trying out for the school team?"

Jacob: (chuckling a bit at your response about the Bulls) "Yeah, I'd like to."

Teacher: "Great. Let me know if you have questions about try-outs. I'd be happy to help in any way."

Jacob: "OK, sounds good. Thanks!" (As Jacob continues towards his seat).

Teacher: (To the remaining students walking into class) "Good morning. Good morning, everyone."

These "micro-conversations" can occur daily as students walk into your classroom (like the examples just described), but they can also occur at appropriate times during class. You'll find that throughout the year there will be natural "pockets" of time when you can engage a student (or group of students) in a "micro-conversation" that might go something like this:

<u>**An example of a "micro-conversation" that is embedded during class time:**</u>

While moving about the room as students work, you recall that your student, Penelope, wrote that if she could eat dinner with anyone it would be Alexander Hamilton.

Teacher: "Hey, Penelope, don't want to get your group off track, but I read your survey where you wrote that you would have dinner with Alexander Hamilton? That's a unique answer. I like it, but I'm curious why you picked Hamilton?"

Penelope: "Well, I really enjoyed social studies last year. We studied the Revolutionary War, the founding fathers, and the Constitution. I was fascinated with Hamilton and his ability to communicate his ideas — especially certain contributions he made to the Federalist Papers."

Teacher: "Wow, that's impressive. Have you always liked social studies?"

Penelope: "Not really. Mrs. Schaeffer made it come alive last year and that made a big difference."

Teacher: "I bet it did. What would you say is your favorite subject – besides mine off course?"

Penelope: (grinning a bit) "I like this class so far. I typically like science, but I really like math."

Teacher: "Wonderful, math and science give people a lot of great opportunities. I remember reading on your survey that you want to be a biomedical engineer."

Penelope: "Yep, my dad is a mechanical engineer, and my mom is a doctor. Biomedical combines the best of both."

Teacher: "That's fantastic. You are well on your way. If I can help in any way, please let me know."

This "micro-conversation" took somewhere between 30-40 seconds. You picked a time in which students were working, but the conversation did not disrupt the learning or productivity of the group. In addition, it allowed Penelope (like Sarah and Jacob previously) to start to realize that you are an advocate for them, you genuinely care about them, and you want to know their hopes, dreams, strengths, even weaknesses, and anything else that makes them tick. **<u>I cannot overstate the value of these micro-conversations</u>**. In my experience, once students realize that you care, they will work for you with zero discipline issues or off-task behavior. I once read something that suggested to picture everyone you meet wearing a sign that reads **"Make me feel important"**. Picture your students wearing that sign. One easy and effective way to let your students know they are important is to consistently engage them in "micro-conversations".

A few more important points about this topic. First, as you now realize, "micro-conversations" don't have to happen only when students enter the classroom. Be aware of a time or two throughout a lesson when you can engage a student without it being disruptive to the productivity of the class. You engaged with Sarah and Jacob as they walked in, but you found time during the lesson to chat with Penelope while still allowing her group to stay on track. Second, be aware not to speak to the same two or three students each day. It might be easier since you already know a little bit about them but doing so might lead to resentment with the others. Distribute your interest in the students equally by engaging with different students each day. As tempting as it may be to continue to focus on the handful that you naturally connect with more quickly, avoid engaging with only those students. Third, use a bit of humor. Notice how in the examples, I mixed in a little bit of humor to lighten the mood. I've found that kids like and appreciate a bit of humor so try to put some into your "micro-conversations". (Sidenote: humor is good, sarcasm can be toxic. A general rule of thumb that I have is "No sarcasm").

You may be thinking "You don't know my students. They won't take the survey seriously and they certainly won't provide answers like Alexander Hamilton". My friendly advice - do not underestimate your students when it comes to giving this survey. Recently I gave this survey to a 3rd grader. For the prompt "If I could have dinner with anyone it would be..." this student wrote "James Madison". Happily surprised, I probed a bit and asked him why he wrote that. He went on to tell me about a website that has books he likes to read and that one of the books he read was about Madison. We went on to chat for a few more minutes. After we concluded our conversation, I reflected to myself and thought what a neat kid he was and how glad I was to have had that chat with him. The bottom line is your students will surprise you in a good way if you allow them. Giving them the survey on day one allows them to do that.

Keep reading the surveys each night. Have your spouse, children, friends, or roommate quiz you. Remember, study your students' answers like you are preparing for the most difficult final exam you've ever taken. Recall the title of this book "Teaching made simple, effective and enjoyable".
This is all about the "enjoyable" part. Engage with your students in a professional, respectful, and friendly way. Get to know your students for the creative, complex, amazing human beings that they are. They have hopes, dreams, fears, strengths,

weaknesses, and lives outside of your classroom. Consistently engaging with them at appropriate times will go a long way towards creating the type of classroom environment that will leave you refreshed and excited to come back every day. It might seem like a daunting challenge at first, but if you have "micro-conversations" with two or three different students every day, you will have chatted with all of them after a few weeks. As the year progresses, keep engaging in "micro-conversations" when appropriate. Doing so will serve to establish a trust and connection with your students that will "make them feel important" (like the invisible sign they are wearing) and will make teaching them the most enjoyable it can be.

Chapter 3 – The next 10 minutes of day one

At this point, all your students have arrived and are completing the student survey that you provided. You want to give them an appropriate amount of time, but not too much time. Do NOT wait until the last person has finished because the rest of the students will potentially get antsy and begin to have conversations with those students nearby. In my experience, students need about 10 minutes to complete the survey, but you can walk about the classroom to get a sense of how close students are to being finished. If most students finish in 10 minutes, collect the completed surveys, and allow the handful of other students to complete it at home. Be sure to have those students turn in their surveys the next day. You need to study all students' answers so that you can begin to have "micro-conversations" with them as soon as possible.

Let's assume you have a class of 30 students and all, but two are finished after 10 minutes. You walk by those two students and realize they still have four "get to know you" prompts plus the last open-ended prompt to complete. At this point you have two options. You could let those two students have five more minutes to complete their surveys while the other students wait, or you could collect all the completed surveys and allow those two students to take their survey home to complete and return the next day. As the teacher, which option would you choose? Option one has an upside because it gives every student the opportunity to complete his or her survey and give it to you that day. The downside is that 28 students would be sitting there with nothing to do for five minutes while those two students finish. You might be thinking – "Five minutes, that's not a long time". Do me a favor and stop reading this book, look at a clock, and sit and do nothing for five minutes. (You don't really have to. I know you get the point). Five minutes of idle time for your students can lead to side conversations and other non-productive activities. Remember, you are setting the tone for your students that they are expected to enter your class and begin working productively and stay productive from "bell to bell". Allowing students to sit idly, even for five minutes, would send the wrong message on the first day.

So, a better choice would be to use your quiet signal (more on the quiet signal in chapter four) and announce:

You: "Eyes and ears on me in three, two, one. Thank you. OK, most of you are finished so I am going to collect your papers. In a minute we are going to practice the quiet signal that I just used, however before I do that, I would like to teach you the procedure for collecting papers".

Q: What is the why for having a procedure for collecting papers?

A: While it's true we are moving more and more towards technology-based teaching, there will most likely always be a need for passing papers to students and collecting papers from students. The more efficient and simpler you make this process, the less likely it is for small disruptions to occur.

As you give the instructions, you should write them on the whiteboard so that students continue to get in the habit of hearing you one time and reading the instructions if necessary.

You: "In this class, the procedure for collecting papers is to pass to your left. If a student is NOT sitting to your left, it is the responsibility of the person that is passing to get up and bring it to the next available student and then immediately return to his or her seat. It is a simple procedure;

however, we are going to practice. I would like you all to pass your surveys to the left." (For the purposes of this initial example, we will assume a traditional classroom set up with desks arranged in rows).

Allow students to correctly demonstrate how to pass the papers in. It is a simple procedure to be sure, but it may be new to students because most teachers have students pass papers forward or backward. Be mindful of how students do. For example, if a student is absent and there is an open seat, watch to make sure the proper person gets up and walks to the next available person. This may seem silly and mundane, but trust me, in the long run you want EVERY student to understand EVERY procedure to a "T".

Assuming the students passed the papers correctly, all the student surveys should be on the far-left desk of each row. ("Left" refers to the students' left and your right as you, the teacher, stand and face your students from the front). You are now ready to announce to the class the last part of the procedure for collecting papers.

You: "Excellent, all the papers are on the far-left desk. Thank you for your attention to this procedure. Now, at this point the student that is seated in the farthest seat to the left and in the back will you please stand up? Young man, what is your name?"

Student: "John Silva."

You: "John, please stand up and grab the stack of papers that you have and please continue towards the front of the room and carefully pick up the papers from the desk in front of you and add that to your stack."

John: (Starts to walk forward) "So, I grab this stack?" (Referring to the stack of papers on the desk directly in front of him).

You: "Yes, exactly. John, please continue to move forward and add the next stack of papers to your current stack."

(John continues walking with a bit more confidence and pace)

You: "Excellent. Thank you, John. Keep coming all the way to the front. There you go – thank you. At this point, John, you have every student's paper. I would like you to take that stack, clip them together, and place them in the tray marked period 1."

(John walks towards the period one tray that you labeled before the year started. There are paper clips near the tray as well).

John: "I put them in the tray?"

You: "Yes, there you go – outstanding. Thank you, John. You may return to your seat."

A question you may have (especially if you are teaching high school students):

Q: "Do I really need to talk and walk students through such a seemingly simple procedure?" Unequivocally, the answer is "YES!" Too often I have seen teachers assume that students will catch on to procedures after hearing them explained one time without practicing. Teachers say, "These kids are ______________" (fill in the blank with any of the following "in high school," "older now," "gifted," "responsible for their actions," etc.) so the teacher does not provide the proper guidance. The teacher assumes that simply talking through the procedure will be enough for all students to understand. Do not assume anything and do not simply talk about your procedures. ___You MUST practice all procedures with your students and have the___

<u>**_students demonstrate exactly what is expected_**</u>.

Students learn best by doing not by simply being told so make sure to practice procedures starting from day one (and keep practicing them throughout the first few weeks if necessary). If you do this, you maximize the chance of creating the most efficient classroom. Think about your own learning – do you learn best by doing or by being told how to do it? The analogy I often use is learning to play a card game. Think about the last time you learned a new game. Did someone read the instructions word for word for 10 minutes while everyone sat there, or did you play a "practice round" to gain a better understanding? I know I learn best by playing that practice round. It is the same for your students. Talking to them for 10 minutes about procedures simply will not be as effective as talking with them as you provide the opportunity for them to practice.

<u>**Two different scenarios that affect passing in papers**</u>

To better illustrate my point of why you should practice procedures consistently and not just talk through them, consider this scenario: You have a classroom of 36 students and your students are seated in six rows with six students in each row. In this example a row is defined as the six desks that go *across* the room. One day, two students, Gwen and Drew, are absent. Gwen sits in the 1st seat of row three. Drew sits in the 5th seat of row four. (See illustration two)

Front of room where you stand and face your students

6th	5th	4th	3rd	2nd	*1st*
					Gwen
6th	5th	4th	3rd	2nd	1st
Ana	Drew	Stefon			

(Illustration two)

Remember, students pass papers to their left, so the fact that Gwen is absent will not affect the process since there are no gaps created by her absence. However, Drew's absence *does* create a gap in the fourth row. Based on the procedure for passing in papers, since Drew is absent, it is Stefon's responsibility (in the fourth seat of that row) to get up and get the papers to Ana (the 6th person in the same row). It is NOT the responsibility of Ana to get up and grab the papers from Stefon. What if Stefon does not remember to get up? The answer is that he slows down the efficiency of this seemingly simple procedure. Consider the potential dialogue that may result:

John: (Waiting to collect the papers from Stefon and Ana's row). "Hey, Stefon, pass those papers please."

(Stefon sits oblivious to the procedure with the papers on his desk. John Silva becomes increasingly impatient and raises his voice).

John: "Hey, Stefon...c'mon, pass those papers!"

(Stefon eventually snaps to and figures out that he should have gotten up and made sure the papers moved to the next person).

Stefon: "Oh, yeah, sorry. Here you go, Ana."

The students in rows one, two, and three do exactly what they should so the stack for their row is ready to be picked up by John. The breakdown occurred because one student, out of 34 in attendance that day, failed to follow the procedure. Therefore, it is imperative that you not only talk to your students about procedures, but that you also allow them to practice, practice, practice. For passing papers in, that would include talking and walking them through different scenarios like the one described above.

Before we move on, I want to address a few more thoughts. The first is about the specific procedure of passing papers in relation to the seating arrangement in your classroom. Teaching science, I had the luxury of having lab style tables in the classroom. I arranged three sets of six lab tables from the front of the room to the back (see illustration three).

Front of room

Table #1	Table #2	Table #3
Table #4	Table #5	Table #6
Table #7	Table #8	Table #9
Table #10	Table #11	Table #12
Table #13	Table #14	Table #15
Table #16	Table #17	Table #18

(Illustration three)

Lab tables were logistically the same as having students in rows. Two students sat at each table facing forward so for all practical purposes this arrangement was the same as the example on the previous page with Gwen, Drew, Stefon, and Ana.

(36 students in a 6 by 6 arrangement). Most of you will have desks (not lab tables) and you might decide to arrange them in rows. If you do, the procedure to pass papers to the left will easily work the same. If you choose to arrange your desks differently, you will have to create a procedure for passing papers that is different from mine. That's perfectly fine. Let's say you decide to group four students together (see illustration four).

Front of room

1	2		1	2
3	4		3	4
1	2		1	2
3	4		3	4
1	2		1	2
3	4		3	4
1	2		1	2
3	4		3	4

(Illustration four)

Having this arrangement means students would not be able to use the "pass to the left" procedure I just described, however there is an equally effective and easy procedure you could teach your students. For this arrangement, all the "twos," "threes," and "fours" would pass their papers to student "one" at their cluster. The "one" at the far left (circled), would grab his group's papers, stand up, and gather the other groups' papers and clip them together to give to the teacher or place in the tray. Simple and effective, right? Whatever you decide, keep it simple and practice, practice, practice this (and all other) procedure(s) with your students.

Another thought I want to share addresses the question:

Q: "Why not just pass papers forward and backward, why pass papers to the left?"

Passing papers forward and backward increases the possibility that a student is not paying attention which ends up with students kicking chairs to get another student's attention or blindly tossing a stack of papers over one's shoulder not knowing if the student behind them is paying attention. The bottom line is that passing papers sideways maximizes the efficiency and simplicity of the task. ***Increased efficiency and simplicity are ALWAYS the goals of EVERY procedure.***

My last thought on this topic is specifically about your students' desks and how you arrange them. There are many ways to arrange seats in a classroom. From traditional rows, desks pushed together, a V-shaped pattern with one half of the room angled one way and the other angled the other, and about any other arrangement you can imagine. I'm not here to say how you should arrange your desks. That's up to you and what you think will help make your students most productive. The bottom line is that you want to create a productive, safe, and engaging learning environment in which all students maximize their learning. For me, that meant putting lab tables in rows because that arrangement maximized learning and productivity in my classroom. There are a variety of arrangements that can create a productive learning environment. There is an upside to moving desks together in groups. If you plan to regularly use cooperative strategies, then desks pushed together might be the most productive arrangement. Just be aware that there is an inherent downside to arranging desks in groups. For example, if students are facing each other, they may be distracted by the person sitting across from them. Potentially this may lead to students paying less attention to you. Typically, there are pros and cons to every arrangement.

Once you create a desk arrangement, try to stick with it. It will be less confusing for your students if you maintain consistency throughout the year. That is not to say you cannot periodically change where students sit. I rearranged the seating chart each quarter so that students could get to know other students in the classroom. Students usually grumbled at first, but they quickly appreciated and enjoyed getting to know other students.

So, change the seating chart from time to time, but find a seating arrangement that maximizes student learning, stick with it, and teach students how to pass papers for that seating arrangement. Now that you and your students have that procedure down, let's turn our attention to another critical procedure – the quiet signal.

Chapter 4 – The quiet signal and the making of a PB & J

Let's recap the first 15-20 minutes of day one. You greeted students professionally at the door, students found their seats on their own, you encouraged them to read the instructions on the board, students completed a survey, and you taught them the procedure for collecting papers. You are now ready to teach them another critical procedure – the quiet signal. You can begin by addressing the students with these words:

You: "Ok, class, thank you for being attentive to the procedure for collecting papers and John, thank you for gathering all of them, clipping them and placing them in the tray. The next procedure we are going to practice is **<u>our</u>** quiet signal."

(Using the word "**our**" sounds better than "**my**" or "**the**" because it implies that the classroom is a unified group of people working towards a common good of learning and productivity).

Q: What is the why for having a quiet signal?

A: Full transparency, this was something I was a bit stubborn about early in my teaching career. The longer I went on, I realized how helpful it was to be able to get everyone's attention on very short notice. This maximized the efficiency of our class and limited the amount of energy I needed to spend getting students quiet when necessary. I eventually saw it as a win-win and students appreciated having something simple in place to get everyone focused.

You: "Throughout the year there will be times when I will need you to give me your undivided attention. For those situations I will be saying 'Eyes and ears on me in three, two, one' and I will raise my hand in the air. When I do this, the expectation is that you stop talking, put your writing utensil down, raise your hand, and turn and make eye contact with me so I know you are fully attentive. (*As you are saying this, remember to write the main points on your whiteboard for students to refer to if necessary*). Now I am going to assign you a shoulder partner and we will practice."

Q: What is the why for assigning each student a shoulder partner?

A: We did a lot of think-pair-share / partner work in my class (especially with vocabulary). Students worked in groups of two or sometimes four. It was helpful to establish that student partnership on day one so that students became accustomed to working together.

At this point, assign partners in which the student seated on the left is the "one" and the student to his or her right is the "two" (See illustration five).

1	2	1	2	1	2
1	2	1	2	1	2
1	2	1	2	1	2
1	2	1	2	1	2
1	2	1	2	1	2
1	2	1	2	1	2

(Illustration five)

As discussed in the last chapter you may choose a different seating arrangement, but that's OK. Regardless of how the students are seated, you can assign a "one" and a "two" for each pair of students. After assigning students a partner you continue to verbally give instructions while also writing instructions on the board.

You: "You all have been assigned a partner. I would like all the "ones" to tell their partner "two" the best method for making a peanut butter and jelly sandwich. Only the "ones" should speak. You have thirty seconds. Begin."

There are three reasons I picked the topic of making a PB & J.

1.) It is a non-academic topic that allows students to practice the quiet signal (the point of this activity is to practice the quiet signal, not make academic gains about an educational topic).

2.) Making a PB & J is something every student is familiar with.

3.) It is something that requires a bit of explaining which will allow students to talk to each other for at least thirty seconds to a minute. If you ask students to "explain to your partner the most enjoyable activity you did this summer" you run the risk of having students shrug to each other and say "I dunno" or "videogames" or "swimming" or other non-descript, one-word answers.

Returning to your lesson, after 30 seconds use the quiet signal to get the students' attention. Check to be sure that all students have stopped talking, raised their hand, and turned to face you. During this initial phase, you should be walking about the room so that students can practice locating you and turning to face you. You may not always be at the front of the room during lessons throughout the year so don't just stand at the front while practicing this procedure. If EVERY student does the procedure correctly, announce something new. If *every* student does not, then announce "Please read the board to be reminded of my expectations. We are going to try again." Most of your students will probably catch on quickly, however sometimes a student will continue talking, forget to put his hand up or forget to turn and face you. ***Do not add anything to the activity until EVERY student does the procedure correctly***.

If your students need to try again, that's OK. Don't single out any students or make a big fuss. You can simply say:

You: "Excellent, most of you followed the procedure. Thank you for being attentive – it shows me you're listening. A few of you did not raise your hand and a few of you forgot to turn and face me so we are going to try it again so that every student demonstrates they understand. "Ones" please continue explaining to the "twos" your method of making a PB & J."

Allow the students to continue and then after only ten seconds announce the quiet signal and see how students respond. Most likely every student will do the procedure correctly this time. When that happens, you are ready to announce the next part of the activity.

You: "Excellent, class I appreciate your effort with this. Student one, you are still doing the talking, but now I would like each of you to list the steps for making a PB & J. You will still work in pairs, and you will both write student one's method on your own sheet of paper. You will have five minutes.

(Remember to set a visible timer for students to see. Additionally, you should write these new instructions on the board. This will continue to reinforce to students that you will say instructions one time).

You: "Class, what are my expectations for the next five minutes." (Wait time of five seconds) — "Alessandra?"

Alessandra: "We are each getting a piece of paper and writing person one's method for making a PB & J."

You: "Excellent. Thank you, Alessandra. You all may begin, and I am setting the timer for five minutes."

Allow students time to write student "one's" method. While students do this, you should be walking about the room listening to conversations for a few seconds and then moving on to the next group. You do not need to interject anything or correct students at all. You simply want to be a presence in the room and use proximity to subtly and non-verbally encourage students to do the task. Occasionally you might say "Excellent" or "Great" or "Nice effort" or "Oh, that's unique I haven't seen another group write that." Begin to show your students that you are a positive force in the classroom and that you are there to encourage them. If for some reason a group chooses not to do the activity do NOT get into a power struggle with them (More on this type of behavior in *Chapter 10 - Stop Grading Papers!*). After two minutes, stop the timer, announce the quiet signal again and wait to make sure that every student responds appropriately. By this time, your students are probably doing well with this procedure, and you can continue with the next announcement.

You: "Eyes and ears on me in three, two, one. Class, I appreciate how attentive you are when I give the quiet signal. I also appreciate the effort – I am hearing some great methods for making a PB & J. Before we continue, I want to add something that I failed to mention earlier. In this class, I would like you to write a heading on all papers. Let's do that together."

(You walk to the board to write down and explain how to write a heading).

Q: What is the why for stopping students and telling them additional steps? Why not just tell them to get a piece of paper and write a heading at the very beginning?

A: Remember, the main point of this part of the lesson is teaching the quiet signal. We are practicing that while at the same time introducing something new. Often times when using the quiet

signal it will be to instruct your students on something you forgot to tell them so introducing something new (like a heading) is good practice for you and for your students.

You: "Students, please write your first and last name in the upper left corner. Below that write Period 1 (or the appropriate period number) and below that you should write the date. All three of those things should be in the upper left corner of your paper any time you write on a piece of paper in our class. The last thing I would like you to include is a title or description of the activity. For today you should write _How to make a peanut butter and jelly sandwich_ on the top line of your paper." (See illustration six)

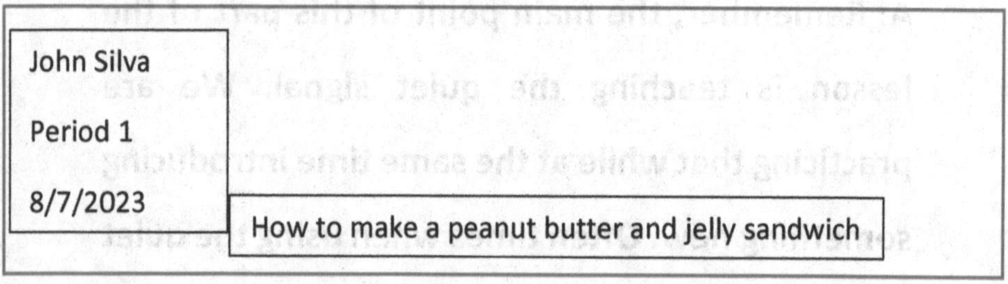

John Silva

Period 1

8/7/2023

How to make a peanut butter and jelly sandwich

(Illustration six)

A few thoughts about the heading:

1.) Students must get in the habit of writing BOTH first and last name. If you have two students named John with the last initial S (John Smith and John Silva) and each of them writes John S on his paper, then you are going to waste time trying to figure out whose paper is whose. Your time and energy are limited – don't waste either.

2.) Throughout the year students may lose or leave papers in your classroom. If students use the correct heading, those papers can be pinned to your corkboard, so they get back to the rightful owner.

3.) Periodically, my students were allowed to use completed assignments and notes on the assessments. Including a date and title will help them determine the subject of each paper AND when it was done. This will allow them to know which papers to use for the assessment (should you choose to make it an open note/handout assessment).

Let's return to your classroom. At this point you have used the quiet signal twice and students have been able to practice while doing a non-academic activity. Refer to the timer that is displayed, start it again, and announce to the students that they have three minutes to complete their steps for making a PB & J. ***After that announcement, continue to move about the room and monitor student work, but be sure to STAY ON TIME***. Too many times I have heard teachers say, "Three more minutes" and then five minutes goes by before the teacher says "Ok, guys just about a minute" and then three more minutes goes by, and the teacher says "OK, guys wrap it up." Seems insignificant, right? Or is it? Think about it: First, you are programming your students that you don't always mean what you say (three more minutes turned into about eight). Second, you are creating a "loose" environment in which students are not expected to maximize their time and stay on task. Your students will rise to the challenge that you set for them. Keep them on time and expect them to work hard. If you say three minutes, then set a timer and stick with three minutes. The only exception is if you say three minutes and realistically every student needed five minutes. In situations like this you can announce "I see you all working hard, and I realize you all need more time; therefore, I am giving you all two more minutes." But be cautious not to get in the habit of allowing more time or your students will come to expect it.

Back to the classroom — the timer is set, and it is counting down. Try to be aware of the time and make periodic announcements ("one minute", "thirty seconds"). If possible, when the last few seconds tick away you can incorporate the quiet signal. It aligns perfectly with the last few seconds ticking down so you could announce "Eyes and ears on me in three, two, one" and raise your hand. By this point, all students should respond appropriately as the timer goes off. You have a few options so let's consider those in the following chapter "Continuing the positive momentum of day one."

Chapter 5 – Continuing the positive momentum of day one

To recap chapter four: You have taught your students the quiet signal while they worked on the non-academic activity of listing the steps to make a PB & J. You have also taught students the proper heading for all papers. From here there are two different paths to go. The biggest consideration is the length of time each class period is. There are typically two types of schedules: 1.) traditional schedule in which each class is in the 50-60-minute range. 2.) block schedule in which each class is in the 70-90-minute range.

<u>Let's first consider a traditional schedule of 55 minutes.</u>

The events so far have taken approximately 30 minutes to complete which means approximately 25 minutes remain. This is the perfect time for your students to take their first assessment. You might be asking – already? To which I respond – absolutely!

Q: What is the why for giving an assessment on day one?

A1.) It will emphasize to students that what they do in class matters.

A2.) It will give you and the students a chance to implement the procedures you have taught them (like writing a heading and collecting papers).

A3.) It will most likely get all the students off to a great academic start.

Here are some sample questions that could be included on your day one assessment (with correct answers in bold):

1.) The quiet signal we use in this class is…

a. Teacher says, "I need everyone quiet now, please."

b. Teacher claps her hands, and the students drop their pencil and clap back.

c. **Teacher says, "Eyes and ears on me in three, two, one."**

d. Teacher says "Class, class" and the students say "Yes, yes."

e. None of the above

2.) When the quiet signal is given, students are expected to

a. stop talking

b. put their writing utensil down

c. turn and face the teacher

d. raise their hand

e. **All the above**

3. When collecting papers in this class, students should...

a. pass to their right

b. **pass to their left**

c. pass forward

d. pass backward

e. None of the above

4. The person responsible for collecting all the papers...

a. will be randomly assigned by the teacher daily

b. will be randomly assigned by the teacher weekly

c. is the person seated in the upper right corner of the room

d. is the person seated in the center of the room

e. **None of the above***

(***the student in the farthest, most left seat is responsible)**

5. The heading on your paper should include...

a. first name and period

b. last name and period

c. first name, last name, and date

d. first name, last name, date, period

e. **first name, last name, date, period, and title of activity**

6. If someone is absent, what is the procedure for passing papers?

a. the teacher will come grab them for that row

b. **the person that is doing the passing is expected to get up and walk them to the next available person**

c. the person that is waiting is expected to get up and get them from the person holding the papers

d. the person holding the papers should continue to pass them forward to the next available person

e. none of the above

Again, these are some sample questions that can be used, but feel free to include other questions related to the first day. The questions should be challenging, but never designed to trick students. The bottom line is that you want to establish to the students that what they learn in your class matters and you, as the teacher, find it important to periodically assess all your students' learning. Prior to giving the quiz, go to the board and write the following:

1.) Please write a heading, including "Quiz #1" on the top line

2.) You will have five minutes to complete the quiz

3.) When you are finished, please turn your paper over and put your pencil down

4.) We will collect your answers and the quiz after five minutes

Use the quiet signal to get every student's attention. Inform them to read the instructions on the board as you explain the process for taking a quiz. Remember, throughout the year, you will say and write instructions one time, so it is critical to continue to write instructions along with giving them verbally.   After instructions, pose the following question to the entire class:

You: "Class, what are my expectations for the next five minutes?" (Always allow wait time of five seconds. If a student blurts out, ignore that student and continue to wait five seconds and call on someone like you normally would).

You: "Thomas?"

Thomas: "We have five minutes to complete the quiz. When we are finished, we should put our pen or pencil down and turn our paper over and wait.

You will collect all the papers at the end of five minutes."

You: "Outstanding, thank you for that Thomas. That shows me you are engaged and attentive today. Those are two things that will benefit all of you this year."

You may be thinking "What if Thomas answers wrong? Or what if Thomas is the class clown and tries to be funny? Or what if Thomas is the kind of student that is so shy that he sits uncomfortably while the rest of the students grow impatient?"

This will be addressed in Chapter 11 – Miscellaneous Q & A

You also may be asking "Should I really check for understanding on such seemingly simple tasks?"

To which I answer – YES! It might seem silly, but the goal of day one is to set the expectation that students pay attention, follow instructions, and

complete what it is you want them to do. In the long run, it will save you and your students time, and it will save your energy.

After Thomas has correctly explained the expectations, you are ready to pass the papers. For passing papers, the procedure was simply the opposite of passing papers in, however there are three considerations to keep in mind.

1.) I started on the students' left and gave the first student enough papers for every student in that row. The first student took one paper and then passed the remaining papers to his or her right. If a student was absent, it was the expectation of the student that had the papers to take one and walk the remaining papers to the next available person. I didn't feel the need to practice this procedure because it was basically the opposite of collecting papers, however, feel free to practice with your students.

2.) I gave students the quiz face down, and I would expect the students to keep them face down until I told them to begin. I didn't think it was fair for any students to get any extra time on the assessment. If five minutes were allotted, then ALL students had five minutes (unless extra time was part of a student's Individual Education Plan, or IEP).

3.) I started at the last row of the classroom and walked backwards toward the front so that I could always keep an eye on every student that had a quiz. If I started at the front of the classroom (which most teachers naturally do) then my back would be facing students as I walked towards the back of the room. I trusted the students, however I just wanted to be sure they weren't tempted to flip the quiz over early.

After handing out the quizzes, you will end up at the front of the room and every student should have the quiz facing upside down on his or her desk. You can switch your timer to five minutes and then announce to the students to flip their quiz over and begin while you start the timer. During quizzes, I liked to stand at the front of the room and observe. I wasn't trying to hover or intimidate, however I felt that I should be a presence during that time. Now was not the time to check emails or do other tasks. This was the time to monitor your students. I also instructed students to come to me if they had a question. I liked to stay in a position where I could keep an eye on all students. If a student had a question and I moved towards that student, it limited my ability to observe the entire class. Most likely students are breezing through this first quiz without any questions or struggles and that's OK. For some of your students, school has been a challenge with very few times of academic success. When they do well on the first quiz, it will provide a bit of a confidence boost. That is not to say that the entire year will be easy, and you are going to "spoon-feed" them an A. But think about it - your students were most likely attentive and on task this first day, which equated to success on the first quiz. The message you have sent to your students is this: "***If you come in and follow the procedures and stay focused, you will be successful.***" I cannot think of a better message to send students on the very first day of school. In my experience, too many students think, "So and so gets good grades because they are smart. I'm not smart so I struggle." It's as if the students that get good grades had some magic pixie dust sprinkled on them. In my opinion, good grades and academic success are about consistent effort. While it may be true that people have different cognitive abilities and academic strengths, it is important that you establish to your students that if they stay focused, follow the procedures, attend school regularly, and put in an honest effort they should be successful.

<u>Back to your classroom</u>:

Your students might be finishing the quiz early or they may need every second. Give them time warnings of "one minute" and "thirty seconds" and then use the quiet signal as the timer ticks down from three - "Eyes and ears on me in three, two, one." Students should follow the expectations including putting their pencil down.

You: "Please pass your answers to the left." (Students should easily follow this procedure since you have already practiced with them).

You: John, please collect all papers, paper clip them and put them in the tray. (John Silva easily collects and paper clips all papers and places them in the period one tray).

You: "Class, please pass the quiz to the left." (Again, John can collect those and put them in the tray, or you might ask him to hand them to you since you will use them again with your next class). At this point, about ten to fifteen minutes remain, and ***you want to teach your students that every minute counts***. You are close to concluding a productive first day with your new students. Now to finish strong!

Chapter 6 – Finishing strong on day one
(traditional 50–60-minute class time)

With the remaining time, I suggest doing an activity called the "Name game." This activity will help you learn the first names of all your students. Someone once told me that the most important word in any language is a person's first name, and I believe that. People like to be addressed by name and that includes your students. The challenge you may face is trying to learn 150-175 new names - a daunting task to be sure even for those with an outstanding memory.

Prior to the "name game", I suggest addressing your students with the following:

You: "I want to call you all by name as soon as possible and I will do my best to learn all your names. I am asking that you are all patient with me. For whatever reason I will learn some of your names quickly, but for others it may take some time. I respectfully request that you please tell me your name if I forget."

I think telling students this did three things:

1.) It genuinely conveyed my feelings about how important it is to address each of them by name.

2.) It established an initial level of trust with your students by conveying *"Each of you matters and I want to respect that"*.

3.) It showed your students that you are human and, consequently, aren't perfect. You will do your best to learn all their names, but you are asking for a bit of understanding from them.

All three of these reasons should help establish trust between you and your students right away.

__The Name Game__

1.) Choose a student to start (the first student seated in the first row is a good place). Let's say that the first student's name is Jacob.

2.) That student says, "My name is Jacob."

3.) The next student (immediately behind Jacob) states "His name is Jacob, and my name is (states her name)." Let's say her name is Tabby.

4.) The third student (behind Tabby) states "His name is Jacob, her name is Tabby, and my name is Alexis."

5.) The student directly behind Alexis states "His name is Jacob, her name is Tabby, her name is Alexis, and my name is Steven."

This continues around the room until the last person has a chance to name every student. This may seem difficult, however in my experience students do well with this. If a student forgets another student's name you can instruct him or her to politely ask "I'm sorry, what is your name?" to which that student can repeat his or her name. Guide students along as they go. As the students repeat the names, you, as the teacher need to focus and take a mental picture of each student. For example, the student named Steven might have a buzz haircut that is the same length ("even"). Since you see Steven and his even haircut you will think "Steven / even." The next time you see Steven (and his "even" haircut) you can address him with a personalized greeting of "Hello Steven, how are you today?" Steven will probably appreciate the fact that you addressed him by name. Try not to use clothing as the connection you use for a student. For example, your new student Jared is wearing red, so you think "Ja<u>red</u> in <u>red</u>." The problem with this is that Jared might not be wearing red tomorrow so the connection or mental image in your mind will not be there. Try to use the physical features of your students (like your student <u>Hurley</u> that has hair that is <u>curly</u>). There won't be a perfect physical description for every student. For some of them you will simply have to try to memorize the face and the name or, like I wrote earlier, you may have to apologize and ask a student to repeat his or her name. If possible, print a seating chart with pictures of students and try to memorize your students' names prior to the year starting. Your students' names will hopefully "stick" even better. Continue to play the name game until the bell rings or stop with about one minute remaining. Hopefully, you were able to get through all your students, however it is not terrible if you did not. You can finish the name game the next day if necessary. An important lesson you are teaching students is that you expect them to use their time wisely and work from bell to bell. If time permits and if every student shared his or her name, you should take a crack at repeating every name. This serves two purposes:

1.) It shows each student you really do care what his or her name is and that you are going to do your best to learn each student's name.

2.) It shows students that you are willing to take risks and attempt to name each student in the class. You may not remember each student's name, but so what? You're likely to learn most of them and your students will appreciate your effort. Besides, you want your students to feel safe to take academic risks throughout the year so who would make a better example on day one than YOU!

The last minute of day one

Hopefully you finished the name game on day one, however like I wrote earlier, you can pause and finish on day two if necessary. Whether you finished or not, with a minute remaining you can announce:

You: "Eyes and ears on me in three, two, one. Thank you. Class, we are off to a fantastic start. I am beyond excited to be working with you this year. You all did a fantastic job today and I look forward to continuing tomorrow. Please pack up quietly and prepare for dismissal. In this class the bell does not dismiss you, I will dismiss you." Students should pack up, sit quietly, and wait while you scan the room for any papers, trash, scraps, or anything else that does not belong. If necessary, you can instruct a student to "please pick up that paper and throw it in the recycle on your way out" or anything else that you deem necessary. Since this is day one, most likely the room is clean, and students are attentive and waiting for you to OK their dismissal. When the bell rings, try not to hold students too long (and never use this time to keep the entire class to punish the group because a few students were disruptive). Quickly check the room and announce, "Push in your chairs and have a wonderful day!" As students leave you can begin placing student surveys on the desks for the next period. When all those papers are on the desks, stand at the door and begin the process again. Take a deep breath and feel great about things. You just created a fantastic start to your year with your first period. But after a deep breath, collect yourself and get ready to do it again with period two. You are now at the door greeting students "Hello, hello, good to see you, welcome. Please read the instructions on the board." The instructions from the first period remain on the board:

Mr./Mrs./Ms. <u>(Teacher's last name)</u>

Welcome to <u>(name of class)</u>

Please find your name on an index card and have a

seat

Please begin filling out the student survey that is

on your desk

You are off to a great start, and you are ready to continue the positive momentum with your next period, but remember they are walking into your room like your first period did approximately 60 minutes ago. Be sure to establish the routines and procedures just like you did in period one. You've already done it once, so this time it will be even smoother. Congratulations! You are laying the foundation for an outstanding year.

Chapter 7 – An alternate strong ending to day one (block schedule)

Let's consider an alternate ending to day one for schools that are on a block schedule (usually 70–90-minute classes). Let's back up to the point where your students are working in pairs ("ones" and "twos") and are writing the steps for making a PB & J. Remember, the events up to this point have taken approximately 30 minutes. That means you have a much larger chunk of time remaining with the block schedule (40-60 minutes). Therefore, my suggestion is to teach your students something academic that will be useful for the entire year – creating a Venn diagram. A Venn diagram is a graphic that allows students to compare and contrast two things. (See illustration seven).

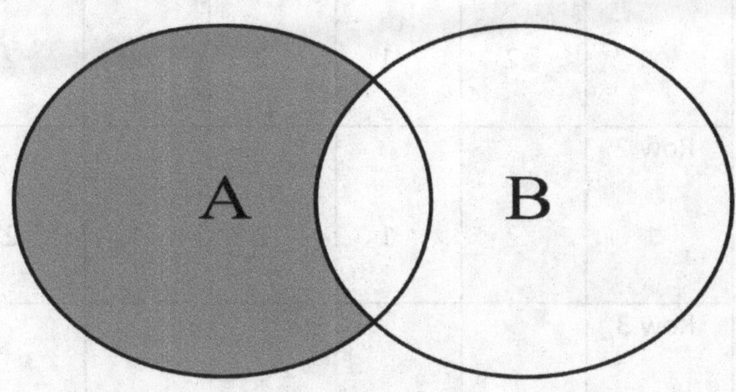

(Illustration seven)

The conversation with your students can go like this:

You: "Eyes and ears on me in three, two, one. At this point I am going to put you into groups of four. I would like the students in the first row to turn and face the students in the second row. Now row three, please turn and face row four. Lastly, row five please turn and face row six. (See illustration eight).

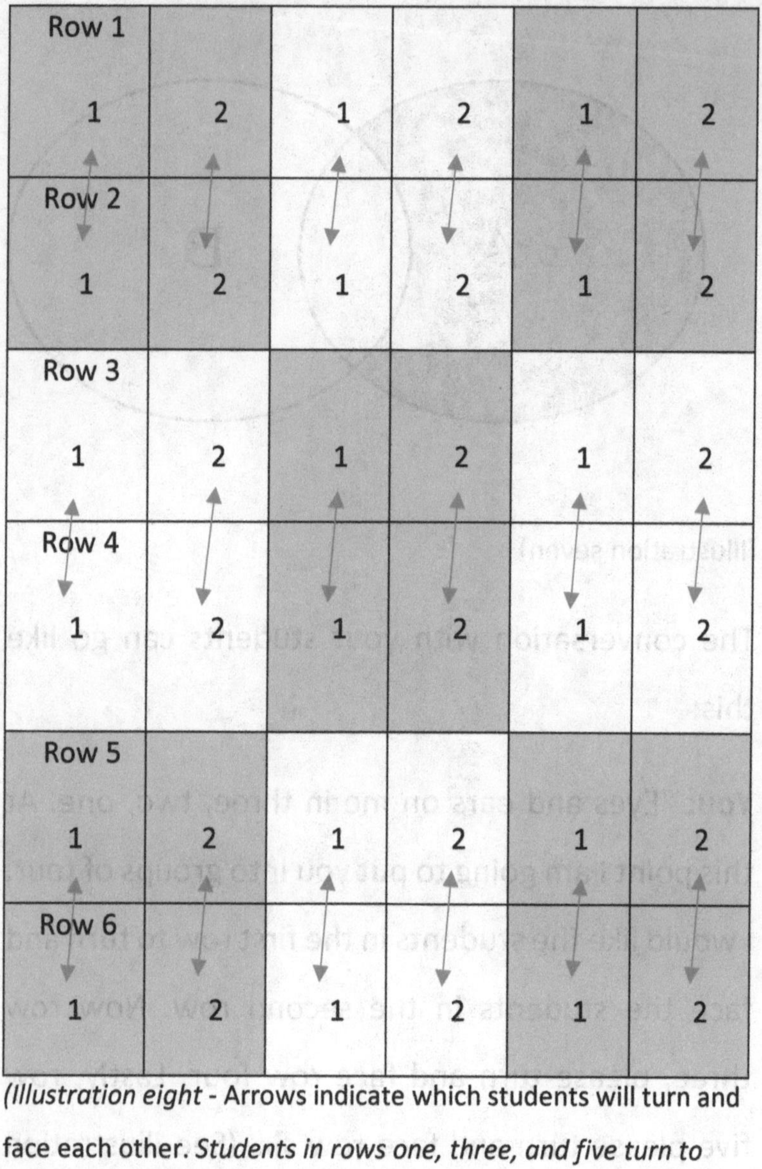

Row 1					
1	2	1	2	1	2
Row 2					
1	2	1	2	1	2
Row 3					
1	2	1	2	1	2
Row 4					
1	2	1	2	1	2
Row 5					
1	2	1	2	1	2
Row 6					
1	2	1	2	1	2

(Illustration eight - Arrows indicate which students will turn and face each other. Students in rows one, three, and five turn to face the students in rows two, four, and six respectively. This creates two pairs of students working in a group of four indicated by the shading and non-shading.

You: "You are now in a group of four – you, your partner, and the pair of students that you are facing. I would like the "twos" to exchange papers" (allow a few seconds for the "twos" to exchange).

You: "Now each pair has two different methods for making a PB & J. You and your partner's method (you walk to one group and hold up one paper), but you also have the method of the group that you are facing (hold up that paper as well). I am going to pass out a paper with a graphic organizer called a Venn diagram. A Venn diagram allows us to compare and contrast. To compare means to find similarities. To contrast means to find differences."

(Remember to write these two words and definitions on the board).

You: "In a minute, I would like each of you to work with only your shoulder partner to complete the Venn diagram. On the far left of the Venn diagram, you should list three things that are unique to you and your shoulder partner's method for making a PB & J. On the far right you should list three things that are unique to the pair of students that you exchanged with. And finally, where the circles intersect you should write three things that both groups have in common for making a PB & J. I am going to model this for you first. Let me take a look at a pair's papers. (You borrow papers from one pair of students). Ok, both groups said they would use a knife to spread the peanut butter and the jelly. Therefore, I am going to write that in the center of my Venn diagram. (You draw a Venn diagram on the whiteboard and in the center, you write *"Both groups used a knife to spread the peanut butter and jelly"*). Ok, now I would like all of you to take one minute and find something to write in the center of your Venn diagram.

After one minute

You: "Eyes and ears on me in three, two, one. Tell me one thing you and the other group have in common. (Wait time of five seconds) Samantha?

Samantha: "Both groups wrote that they would use two pieces of bread."

You: "Excellent, that would go in the center of your Venn Diagram." Class let's practice one more. Write one thing that would go on the left side of the Venn diagram and write one thing that would go on the right side. Remember that the far left is something unique to your group and the far right is something unique to the other group. I'll give you two minutes." (Keep writing your instructions on the board each time you give verbal instructions and continue to check with one student in the class to explain what your expectations are for the upcoming activity. Also, always set a timer so students stay on time).

(After two minutes)

You: "Eyes and ears on me in three, two, one. What is something you wrote on the left side of the Venn and what is something you wrote on the right side? (Wait time of five seconds) Darcy?"

Darcy: "On the left side, we wrote that we would put the jelly on only one piece of bread and the peanut butter on the other. The other group would put peanut butter and jelly on both pieces, so we wrote that on the right side."

You: "Excellent. That's exactly how this works. Thank you for sharing that. Class, please be prepared to summarize how we use a Venn diagram." (Wait time of five seconds) Shondra?"

Shondra: "There are three parts of a Venn diagram. On the left side we write what is unique to our group, on the right side we write what is unique to the other group, and in the center, we write what is common to both groups."

(As Shondra is answering, you should label each part of the Venn diagram you wrote on the board earlier).

You: "Wonderful, great description. Again, we are using the center to compare, which means to find similarities and we are using the two outside parts of the Venn to contrast which means to find differences. For the next five minutes I would like you to complete the Venn diagram by writing two more statements in each of the three sections. That would give you a total of three in each section. (*Write those instructions on the board and set your timer for five minutes*). I would like one student to tell the class my expectations for the next five minutes. (Wait time of five seconds) Juana?"

Juana: "On the left side of the Venn we are to write two more things that are unique to our method and on right side we are going to write two more that are unique to the other group's method. In the middle where the circles intersect, we should list two more that we both included."

You: "Excellent Juana. That is a fantastic description. Thank you for being focused. Class, the timer is running, you may begin."

Q: What is the why for introducing the Venn diagram on day one?

A: Comparing and contrasting is an excellent way for students to engage in higher level thinking. The Venn diagram is a graphic organizer that easily allows students to compare and contrast. It can be something you and your students use throughout the year. By teaching students how to use it with a non-academic activity (making a PB

& J), students will more easily be able to use it when you begin to teach academic content.

A Venn diagram by itself doesn't make great instruction, however it is a useful tool that you and your students can use throughout the year. Equally important, you are setting the tone with your students from day one, that when they come to your class, they will be expected to learn and be productive. This is such a critical takeaway that your students need to know.

After five minutes, you can go over a few of the students' Venn diagrams to make sure that everyone in the class understands how to use one. After that, there should be approximately 20 minutes remaining so it would be logical to finish this block schedule exactly how we finished the last 20 minutes of the traditional schedule: pass out the quiz, students take the quiz (be sure to remind students about the heading), collect the quiz, play the name game, students pack up, and you dismiss them. One minor change is that the quiz for a block class should include questions about a Venn diagram since the block schedule students learned how to use it.

Recap of day one for both traditional and block schedule

Each period of the day your students were productive from the minute they walked in. Your students completed a survey, and you collected those surveys so you can get to know your students and begin to engage in micro-conversations throughout the year. Additionally, your students learned and practiced a few procedures including the quiet signal, passing papers, and how to write a heading. Furthermore, students in the block schedule learned how to use a useful graphic organizer called a Venn diagram. Students took their first quiz, and they were probably successful, which sent a message that being attentive leads to success. Lastly, you had a chance to learn the most important word in any language – each student's name. You had bell to bell instruction, and you established a solid foundation for "doing business" in your classroom. Congratulations! I cannot think of a better way to start day one of a new school year. Remember my goal for you – ***_I want your first day to be productive and enjoyable, but I want your last day, and every day in between, to be the same_***. I am confident it can be done, and now you are well on your way to doing that!

Chapter 8 – Creating engaging and effective lessons

A lesson plan should allow a teacher to create a pathway for his or her students to move toward and eventually meet the objective. That's it – nothing more, nothing less. I have seen several lesson plan templates. Most are complicated and difficult to complete. Some templates require teachers to fill in all sorts of categories and boxes and possibly even scripted instruction. That is simply not an effective or sustainable way to write lessons. Don't get me wrong, if a teacher is to be as effective as possible, he or she *should* write a plan, but if it is overly time consuming, the teacher will be hard pressed to consistently write them. Fortunately, the following lesson plan design is both simple and effective with a framework that guides a teacher but allows for creativity. A teacher should be able to write a lesson in 10-15 minutes using the following lesson plan format. On the following page, I have included an actual lesson plan that I created for a cell cycle lesson when I taught biology. I thought it would be helpful for you to see a finished lesson plan prior to looking at the specifics of how to create it.

<u>Lesson plan template</u>:

Final objective

Sub-objective #1

Aligned activity #1

Sub-objective #2

Aligned activity #2

Sub-objective #3

Aligned activity #3

Final objective + final aligned activity

Cell cycle lesson plan

<u>**Final objective**</u>: *"The student will demonstrate **understanding** of the cell cycle by **summarizing** the sequence of events using the terms replication, alignment, and separation."*

Sub-objective #1 – The student will demonstrate **knowledge** of the cell cycle by **identifying** the phase for each slide.

Aligned activity #1 – The students will write the name of each phase of the cell cycle for each of the prepared onion root tip slides that the teacher shows the class.

Sub-objective #2 – The student will demonstrate **application** of the cell cycle by **drawing** each stage.

Aligned activity #2 – Students will draw and label the stages of the cell cycle on a sheet of notebook paper.

Sub-objective #3 – The student will demonstrate **analysis** of **the cell cycle** by **categorizing** six unlabeled pictures.

Aligned activity #3 – The teacher will give each student six pictures of the cell cycle in random order. The students will place the pictures in the correct sequence.

Final objective + final activity - The student will demonstrate **understanding** of **the cell cycle** by **summarizing** the sequence of events using the terms replication, alignment, and separation.

Template with notes describing each section:

Final objective - *Start with the end in mind; What skill or standard do you want students to learn? The final objective and all sub-objectives are written in a specific format that you will read about in the next few pages.*

Sub-objective #1 - *Sub-objectives are the steps that are needed to get to the final objective and are written in the same format as the overall objective. Typically, a lesson plan has three sub-objectives, however some may have more depending on the lesson. Sub-objective #1 would be the first step toward the final objective.*

Aligned activity #1 - *Every sub-objective has an aligned activity. Each activity may take varying amounts of time depending upon the complexity of the sub-objective. Aligned activity #1 is designed to help students meet sub-objective #1.*

Sub-objective #2 - *This is the next step toward the final objective.*

Aligned activity #2 - *Aligned activity #2 is designed to help students meet sub-objective #2.*

Sub-objective #3 – *This is the next step toward the final objective. In the case of this lesson, it would be the last sub-objective before students work on the final objective and final activity.*

Aligned activity #3 – *Aligned activity #3 is designed to help students meet sub-objective #3.*

Final objective + final aligned activity - *Every lesson plan starts and ends with the same final objective. By the end of the lesson all students should be expected to __DO__ something which will be the evidence you need to know that they have met the objective.*

Now that you have seen the overall lesson plan design, let's look at the formula for writing both final objectives and sub-objectives.

The student will demonstrate (_insert Bloom's taxonomy* level_ here) of (insert _content_ here) by (insert Bloom's _verb_ here).

***Bloom's taxonomy was created by Benjamin Bloom in 1956. See a creative commons version of Bloom's taxonomy below.**

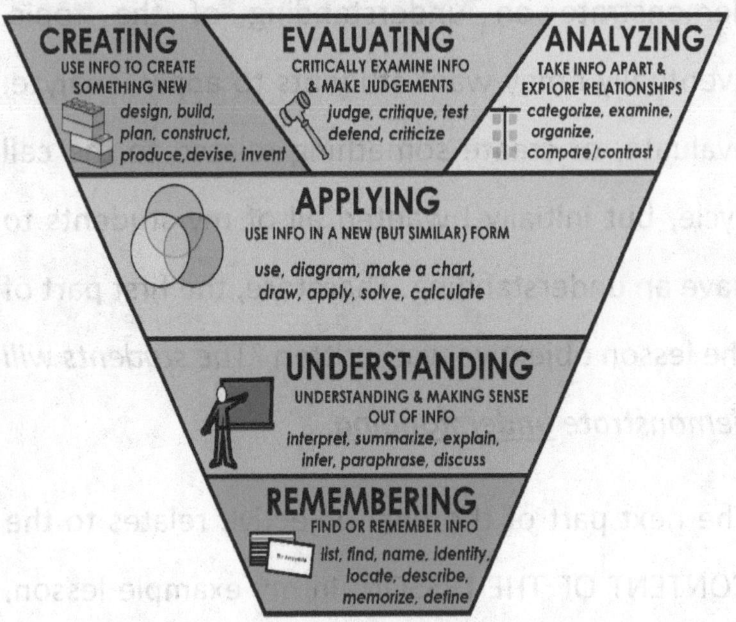

Let's walk through the steps used to create my cell cycle lesson from the previous page. Every objective starts with the same prompt **"The student will demonstrate...".** Using Bloom's taxonomy, I needed to determine what level of Bloom's taxonomy I wanted my students to reach. In other words, did I want students to Remember? Understand? Apply? Analyze? Evaluate? Or Create? Since this was their first introduction to the cell cycle, it was fitting for my students to demonstrate an understanding of the topic. Eventually I may want students to apply, analyze, evaluate, or create something related to the cell cycle, but initially I wanted all of my students to have an understanding. Therefore, the first part of the lesson objective was written "T*he students will demonstrate **understanding**...*"

The next part of the final objective relates to the CONTENT OF THE LESSON. In my example lesson, the content was the cell cycle. Therefore, I added to the objective so that it now read *"The student will demonstrate understanding of **the cell cycle**..."*

To complete this lesson objective, I had to determine what action I wanted my students to do to demonstrate they had met the objective. That action is always a verb taken from the level of Bloom's taxonomy written in the first part of the objective. Since students were expected to understand the cell cycle, the verb *"**summarize**"* was chosen from the "understanding" level. Now that I knew all three components of the formula, Bloom's level + content + Bloom's verb, I was ready to write the final lesson objective.

*"The student will demonstrate **understanding** of **the cell cycle** by **summarizing** the sequence of events using the terms replication, alignment, and separation."*

To recap – for this final objective: Bloom's taxonomy level is understanding, the content is the cell cycle, and the students were expected to demonstrate evidence of understanding by writing a summary. Again, the final objective is written with the end in mind. Keep it simple and always remember these two questions: **What standard (or skill) do you want students to learn? What evidence will you have that they have learned it?**

My hope is that you are starting to see the ease with which lesson objectives can be written by choosing the level of Bloom's taxonomy, the content from the standards you teach, and a verb from the Bloom's level that you want your students to achieve.

Now that we know how to write a final objective, let's consider how to get students toward that final objective by creating sub-objectives and aligned activities. I will now explain the three sub-objectives and the aligned activities for each sub-objective from the cell cycle lesson that I taught my students. I included notes in parentheses to reinforce the ease with which this process can be completed.

Final objective: *"The students will demonstrate **understanding** of **the cell cycle** by **summarizing** the sequence of events using the terms replication, alignment, and separation."*

Sub-objective #1 – The students will demonstrate **remembering** of **the cell cycle** by **identifying** the phase for each slide. (*All students needed a foundation of each phase of the cell cycle, therefore the lesson started at the knowledge level. The verb "identify" was selected since it is found in Bloom's level of remembering*).

Aligned activity #1 – The students will write the name of each phase of the cell cycle for each of the prepared onion root tip slides that the teacher shows the class. (*Students were shown 36 onion root tip slides, one at a time, from an online program and asked to identify each. For the first few slides, I modeled for them by choosing the correct phase and explaining why I chose that particular phase. I continued to show students slides, but now students were called upon individually to explain their choice. Students wrote down the agreed upon choice. As more students demonstrated understanding, each "one" told his or her partner "two" an answer and wrote it down. Students were asked to explain their choice and the rest of the students were allowed to agree or disagree with that choice and verbalize their reasoning. Eventually as all students demonstrated proficiency with this task, the students gave a choral response until all 36 slides had been identified and the phase for each had been written).*

Sub-objective #2 – The student will demonstrate **application** of **the cell cycle** by **drawing** each stage.

Aligned activity #2 – Students will work individually to draw each phase of the cell cycle in their notebooks. (*The verb "draw" was used because it is found within Bloom's level of application. Students spent 10 minutes drawing each phase of the cell cycle and then compared their drawing with their partner. Students engaged in a class discussion about what a correct drawing should include. Students were able to use both the comparison with their partner and the ensuing discussion to make any necessary changes to their drawing).*

Sub-objective #3 – The student will demonstrate **analysis** of **the cell cycle** by **categorizing** six unlabeled pictures.

Activity #3 – The teacher will give each student six pictures of the cell cycle in random order. The students will place the pictures in the correct sequence. *(I photocopied six unlabeled pictures of each phase of the cell cycle and gave one set to each student. Students worked individually to place those pictures in the correct sequence but were given time to check their work with their partner and the students near them. The verb "categorize" was selected because it is found within Bloom's level of analysis. A class discussion ensued in which I randomly selected students to answer questions regarding not only the sequence, but how they determined that sequence. Students were allowed to ask clarifying questions if necessary.)*

Final objective – The student will demonstrate **understanding** of **the cell cycle** by **summarizing** the sequence of events using the terms replication, alignment, and separation.

After the students had completed the three aligned activities with the teacher and classmates, each student wrote a summary of the cell cycle. The students included the terms replication, alignment, and separation. This final activity took about ten minutes for students to complete. A timer was set to encourage students to complete this task in the allotted amount of time. After ten minutes, I chose a few students to share what they had written. Students were encouraged by me to "read exactly what you wrote". Some students had accurate summaries, but some did not. That's OK. We used that time to correct any misconceptions and make sure all students had a clear understanding of the final objective.

To recap some thoughts about this lesson. First, always start with the end in mind and think about what it is you want **your students to be able to do by the end of the lesson** to demonstrate they have met the objective. Second, the sub-objectives and aligned activities are scaffolded and designed to move students toward the final objective. Remember, students should periodically be expected to DO something throughout the lesson. This helps you know if your students are moving towards the final objective. As students do each aligned activity, take time to walk about the room to encourage, guide, and support your students and then be sure to discuss the students' results after each activity. Doing this will give you a better sense if students have met each sub-objective, which ultimately will guide them towards the final objective. If students attempt an aligned activity and you notice that the majority did not do well or are confused on what to do, stop and revisit that activity. Sometimes, stopping and going back to re-explain part of the lesson is exactly what students need. In some cases, you might have to set up a different activity altogether. The point is that you want your students to have a clear understanding of what to do for each aligned activity AND have a clear understanding of how that activity relates to learning the sub-objective associated with it. This will help ensure that they have met the sub-objective that you created which will be your indication to move on to the next sub-objective and aligned activity.

Second, carefully consider the sequence of sub-objectives and aligned activities. Notice how I started with a sub-objective at the remembering level then moved to the second sub-objective at the application level and then lastly to the analysis level in sub-objective #3. The level of Bloom's taxonomy that I was expecting the students to ultimately achieve dictated the sequence. That is not to say that every first sub-objective will be at the remembering level. Nor does it mean that your students will always move towards analysis, evaluation, or synthesis. It simply means that you will scaffold your lessons in a logical and appropriate sequence. Again, this process is designed to give you the freedom, flexibility, and creativity to get your students where they need to go. Think of yourself as the conductor of an orchestra. Just like a conductor guides, encourages, and supports in a creative way, a teacher does the same.

Before we wrap up the cell cycle lesson and this chapter, I want to emphasis one of the most important ideas for teachers to believe. **<u>It is absolutely critical that the students work harder than you during your lessons.</u>** That may sound strange, and, truth be told, I had a hard time with this when I first started teaching, but eventually I realized how important it is that the students work harder than me during class. To avoid burnout, you

MUST create lessons in which students regularly demonstrate learning by doing something throughout the lesson. The majority of a teacher's work should be done in the preparation of a lesson, NOT during the lesson. Sometimes that is a hard thing for teachers to realize and accept, but I offer that advice in the friendliest way. Remember, I want you to go home excited and invigorated each day. I feel strongly that teachers setting up lessons in which they do the majority of the work rather than the students is a major contributing factor to teacher burnout. So, please use your prep time to create lessons designed to allow students to do the majority of the work during class. Remember, students should be expected to regularly and periodically **DO** something throughout each lesson which becomes evidence of their learning.

I hope this chapter has given you a solid understanding of an especially important process.

Lesson plan design is critical, but it doesn't have to be agonizing or difficult. I believe teachers can actually enjoy and look forward to this process. Like anything else, as you practice, you will become increasingly adept at it. My hope is that you will be creating effective and engaging lesson plans in about 15 minutes. (Imagine creating a lesson plan in 15 minutes!) My suggested template allows and encourages you to use your creativity to develop more meaningful and engaging lessons that lead students toward deeper learning. Ok, maestro - it's your orchestra! Have fun and conduct your students where you want them to go!

Chapter 9 – Day two and beyond

Hopefully, you feel great about the start of your year and how things went on day one. You accomplished a lot, and you are ready to continue the positive momentum. Day two and beyond you should follow a simple routine that will put students in a position to be successful. Some people hear the word routine and think "boring." I hear the word routine and think "smart and productive." In my experience, students like routine. They do well when they clearly know what the expectations are. Therefore, with a few exceptions, you should begin every day the exact same way. This will establish an excellent routine that will help your students be the best they can be.

<u>**Establishing a daily routine**</u>

Every day when students enter your classroom, there should be a 3-5 question warm-up on the board. These questions should be related to the lesson from the previous day or the last few days. The questions should be challenging, but simple and straightforward enough to get students thinking about your class again.

Q: What is the why for giving a warmup every day?

The following reasons explain why it is essential to give a daily warm up:

A1.) Students are seated and productive from the first second of the class period.

A2.) It gets students thinking about what they learned from the previous day(s).

A3.) It allows you time to take attendance.

A4.) It sends a message to your students that every minute counts and when they come into your classroom it is time to work.

Let's consider some warm-up questions for your students on day two.

1.) What is the quiet signal we will use in this class?

2.) What are my expectations for students when I say the quiet signal?

3.) What is the procedure for passing in papers?

4.) What is the expectation when passing papers if someone is absent (who gets up?).

5. What is the purpose of a Venn diagram? (For the block class)

Notice how these questions are related to the previous day's content. They are also simple and straightforward. The warmup is not intended to stump students, but to get them in a productive, working mode thinking about the content of your class. Set the timer for two minutes and stay on time! Keep in mind that you do not have to wait until the last person is finished. Students will rise to the expectation that you set so give them an appropriate amount of time and then stick with that time. For the warmup example above, two minutes is sufficient for your students. Other warmups may require slightly more time, however, the warmup should never be more than five minutes. I've seen teachers give ten or even twenty minutes on a warmup. This is entirely too much time! Remember, you are training students to work bell to bell and that every minute counts. Two to five minutes should always be sufficient, so, again, set the timer and stay on time. When the timer goes off, announce the quiet signal, and pause to make sure that every student has stopped, put his or her pencil down, has his or her hand up and is facing you. You are most likely at the front of the room so basically the students should be attentively facing forward. Call on five different students to answer each warmup question. This should be a quick process. You can stand at the board and write each student's response as he or she gives you the answer. It is likely that students will give you the correct answer since warm up questions are not designed to stump students. After the first student answers correctly respond by encouraging them ("Fantastic, that was an excellent answer"). You don't have to be overly dramatic and sappy, but you do want to continue to show your students that you are a positive force in the classroom and that you are always there to encourage and support them.

A couple other considerations about the warmup:

1.) During the warmup, what if students ask clarifying questions?

Occasionally students will ask questions based upon the conversation that ensues from the warmup. When this occurs, my suggestion is to answer those questions in a timely manner so that students have a clear understanding of each answer.

2.) During the warmup, what if a student asks an excellent question that is not completely related to the topic and may require more time to explain?

Sometimes students will ask thoughtful questions that would genuinely enhance the learning of all students but would require more time to explain or aren't completely related to the learning objective. If this occurred, I would write the question in the "parking lot" (a long piece of butcher paper taped on the wall). All students had one day to research the question, write a half page summary, cite the resource, and present the information in one minute or less to the class the following day. If multiple students had a prepared answer the next day, I typically had one or two students read to the class and collected the rest. The overall idea of the "parking lot" is to allow students to be inquisitive and genuinely seek answers to questions they have, while allowing you to keep the class focused on the daily objective.

3.) What if a student asks a silly question or seeks superfluous information that would sidetrack you and take the class away from the learning objective?

Keep in mind that not every question needs to be answered immediately or be written in the "parking lot." Some questions may be so random that they are best if ignored. Some students might pose silly, off-topic questions designed to get you off track. It may not happen often or at all, but it might happen. Please don't misunderstand me, questions from students are usually good, however you will start to understand the difference between on topic questions that you can answer quickly, excellent questions that might take too long (so they get "parked" and answered the next day by either you or a student), and random questions asked by students that are trying to get you off topic and delay the start of the lesson.

Continuing day two

You have given the warm-up, taken attendance, and called on students to answer. This process has taken five to seven minutes depending on the length of time you gave students to answer the warmup. You are now ready to go into the next part of your daily routine – vocabulary. Vocabulary is a critical part of any course, so have your students spend five minutes reviewing vocabulary every day. During this time, I found tremendous success having each "one" work with his or her partner "two". Vocabulary can be difficult for students and having them work in pairs seemed to allow them to take more risks than if we worked on vocabulary in a whole group. Overall, students working in pairs led to outstanding vocabulary comprehension for my students. After a review of vocabulary, teach the lesson plan that you have created for that day. Remember from chapter eight that you should have an overall objective, and sub-objectives and aligned activities as well. As a reminder, students should be required to do something to demonstrate their learning (in other words, you know students have met the objective by seeing something that they produce). ***Lastly, remember to leave five to ten minutes at the end of each lesson to have a student or a group of students share their final product***. Then allow a few minutes for students to ask clarifying questions. Depending on how students do and the clarifying questions they ask, you may want to spend a few minutes reteaching. Or if all the students have met the objective, call on one or two of them to summarize their learning. As you get further along in your career, you will develop a "feel" for how your students did overall with that day's objective. Some lessons will go exactly the way you want, and some will not. That is the nature of this profession. Depending on how a lesson goes, you can respond accordingly. Obviously, my hope is that students meet the lesson objective every day, but the reality is that there will be days when you will re-teach parts of a lesson to the entire class, work with a small group of students, or group students together so they can work to support each other.

Two friendly pieces of advice about each lesson:

1.) Give yourself a bit of grace. If a lesson doesn't go exactly how you want, it's OK!

Adjust during the period or from one period to the next. If necessary, reteach the lesson the next day using different sub-objectives and aligned activities.

2.) Teach less, better. Take your time and go a bit deeper with fewer concepts each day. I've heard over and over that teachers feel rushed to "cover the curriculum". In an effort to do that, teachers speed through too many concepts which results in students actually learning less.

Back to our routine. Most days will follow the same overall structure – warmup, vocab practice, teach the daily lesson, then students summarize their learning. Again, routine does not equal boring. Routine equals smart and productive! In my experience, students will quickly get used to this routine and they will absolutely flourish because of it.

After students summarize the learning for the day, they can pack up, sit quietly, and wait for the bell. During this time, I would state some positive thoughts for the class. "This class is off to a great start so far this year. I am excited to see all the progress you will make" or "Overall, this class is doing wonderfully. I appreciate you all coming in, staying focused and working hard." As often as possible (every day if you can), give your students a positive feeling as they leave. Like I wrote earlier, NEVER hold the entire class back when the bell rings because a handful of students misbehaved. Deal with individual student misbehavior as it occurs. (In my experience, I did not deal with much misbehavior since I had established trust between myself and my students by calling each of them by name, regularly engaging in "micro-conversations" and by being a positive force and advocate for all of them). The last half minute should always include a positive message about that day and an excitement to see them again. Have students check for scraps of paper or any garbage and politely request that students help keep our (***our and not my***) classroom clean. When a student stoops down to grab a piece of paper make sure to respond with "Thank you (calling that student by name). I appreciate you being courteous and respectful." Always model the way you want students to speak and interact. It is important for them to hear that, and it is important for them to hear you acknowledge them. It will continue to build trust in the teacher – student relationship which will serve to bolster that positive productive culture you have established in your classroom. Eventually the bell will ring, but remember YOU dismiss students. After checking the room one last time, you can announce "Thank you. You may push in your chairs and leave. Have a wonderful day!"

If possible, stand near the door to greet the next group of students (engage in a couple "micro-conversations" while you are there), but be sure to re-write the warm-up (and erase any answers from the board) and write any instructions for the next group (remember you write instructions and say them once).

Congratulations! You have just completed day two. Day three will follow in the same overall structure of day two: a warm-up, vocabulary, and a lesson plan that leads toward the objective. Day four will follow in the same format, as will days five, six, seven all the way until the last day of the year. I know some of you are thinking: **"Can teaching really be this simple?" The answer is: (A resounding) "YES!"**

Remember, the title of this book <u>"Teaching made simple, effective, and enjoyable"</u> and remember the words I wrote on the first page:

I want your first day to be productive and enjoyable, but I want your last day, and every day in between, to be the same. Sound impossible? I'm here to tell you it's NOT.

Now you know why I wrote that it's possible to make day one, the last day and EVERY day in between productive and enjoyable. It can be done, and YOU can do it!

Chapter 10 – Stop grading papers!

The following sentence is going to shock some of you. Stop grading papers! Yes, I wrote it – Stop grading papers! Some of you may remember a song by John Lennon called "Imagine." Lennon opines how much better life would be without countries, possessions, and religion among other things. I'm not saying Lennon is right. I'm simply referencing a song that makes one stop and think. I present the idea to stop grading papers in the same way. Imagine if you did not grade one paper the entire year. How would that change your year? I know what some of you are thinking: ***<u>But I'm a teacher, that's what I do. How would I know how my students are doing? How would I assign grades?</u>***

Allow me to clarify. Notice that I didn't say, "Stop assessing student learning" or "stop giving grades." You can still do both. Formative and summative assessments will still be embedded throughout the year and students will still earn a grade. Remember what I am suggesting – ***stop grading papers.***

Q: What is the why for not grading papers?

Allow me to give you a sports analogy to explain why. I coached basketball for several years. We had practice on a regular basis (daily, except for game days, Sundays, and holidays). When we practiced, players worked on fundamental skills and team concepts. It was up to all of us (coaches and players) to work as hard as we could to prepare for the upcoming game. But the bottom line is that we were not assessed for our practices. In other words, no one came into the gym and rated our practice or gave us points based on how hard we worked. No matter how we practiced prior to a game, at tipoff the score was always 0-0. What's my point? The daily activities within the classroom are just that – practice. ***The daily lessons of our classrooms should be treated just like practice***

<u>*sessions in the gym.*</u> Students should give maximum effort, be encouraged by the teacher, be guided and corrected when appropriate, discuss the answers with classmates and the teacher, and encourage each other as well. This should all be done with the intention of learning the concepts for the weekly or bi-weekly assessment. Basically, the daily classroom activities are like practice and the assessments are the games. Just like no one is in the gym giving our team points for how we practice, no one should give students points for how well they complete daily classroom activities. The points will be given when the student takes the assessment that allows them to demonstrate learning. Seem impossible? Please believe me – it is not. The reason I know this is because I did this for the last few years of my teaching career.

Classroom in which everything is collected for grading

Let's consider a typical lesson given on a Tuesday in the middle of October: Teacher assigns reading and questions from the text, students work individually or in groups to read and answer questions, students work until the bell, and students rush to hand papers in so they can get points. Think about that for one minute. What has this scenario created? A huge pile of papers that the teacher must grade. If each class has 30 students, and the teacher teaches five periods, he or she is now responsible for grading 150 papers later that day or evening. And let's face it, how much feedback can a teacher give students when he or she is trying to get through 150 papers. Too often, the teacher hurriedly and sloppily writes a +5 or +10 on the top of the paper to quickly get through the stack. In addition, usually that pile of papers isn't returned to students for days or even weeks which makes any feedback (if it were even included) meaningless.

Classroom in which papers are not collected

Now imagine a different scenario. The teacher gives the assignment. The students use class time individually or in groups to get the assignment done. The teacher saves 10 minutes to discuss answers with the students. (***Remember, you always want to leave time at the end of the lesson for students to demonstrate their learning***). The teacher has students provide the answers they found from reading. The teacher corrects misconceptions. The students make necessary changes so that all answers are correct. Then the biggest shift – rather than turning that work in to the teacher, ***the students keep the assignment in their notebooks, folders, or computer.*** The following day the teacher provides a warm-up, has the students practice the vocabulary, and teaches the lesson based on the daily lesson plan that he or she created. Later in the week (usually every Friday or every other Friday), the teacher provides an assessment designed to determine how well the students have mastered the skills and standards that were taught throughout the week. Based on the results of the assessment, you have a few options: If all students did well, you can move to the next topic or unit. If most students did well, but a few did not, you can work with that group during study hall or another time (before or after school, during a pocket of time in class, etc.). If the majority did not do well, you might consider reteaching the entire class using different sub-objectives and aligned activities. The bottom line is that the assessments help you know if students are learning the skills and standards that your daily objectives are intended to help them learn. You don't collect papers, but you do give weekly or bi-weekly assessments to gauge true student learning. The daily lessons are like practice, the assessment is like the game.

Addressing any misconceptions about this radical shift in thinking

At this point I would like to address some doubts that you might have because I had the same doubts (misconceptions) prior to trying this system.

Misconception #1: Students won't do the work.

I found the complete opposite to be true. In fact, my students did more work when I stopped collecting papers. It took all the pressure off students and allowed them to work knowing that we were all in this together. They knew that later in the period they would be sharing answers and that eventually I would be helping them fill in any missing gaps in knowledge that they had. They appreciated that and actually worked harder.

Misconception #2: Students will still want to turn papers in.

I had a few students ask, "Are we turning this into you at the end?" to which I always replied "No, but don't forget you'll need it for the quiz on Friday." After two weeks students completely stopped asking. From the beginning of the school year, I made it clear to my students that I would not be collecting worksheets, handouts, pages from their notebooks, warmups, or any other classwork that they did. I explained this system during the first week when I discussed the syllabus. Again, after two weeks, not one student asked, "Are you collecting this?"

Misconception #3: Students will learn less.

Again, I found the opposite to be true. My classroom became a safe place of learning and discovery. Students knew that what they did mattered because the concepts would be on the weekly assessment. Besides, think about the earlier example I wrote in which students read a passage in the textbook, write answers on a sheet of paper, and then turn in the answers at the end of the period. How do we know students have truly learned the concepts and standards that we want them to learn? The bottom line is we don't, and yet we spend hours giving students points for doing things that may or may not demonstrate learning. The better way to know if learning has taken place is to provide an assessment later in the week to see what the child knows. It's like my basketball analogy earlier. The only way to truly assess my team was to have them play a game. Only then can I, as the coach, know if players are learning the fundamental skills and team concepts that we are implementing in practice. I always told people, _**"If I thought students were learning less or this system**_

in any way minimizes learning, I wouldn't do it."

But the fact is, I found the opposite to be true.

I have two last points to make about this system.

1.) Become a positive force in your classroom

This system frees up the teacher to become a positive force in the classroom. Rather than pestering the apathetic student that isn't doing the work, you can focus on the majority that are. It is physically and mentally draining to try to get someone to do something that he or she does not want to do. Prior to this radical shift, I spent time saying to some students, "take out your pencil", "c'mon get something on this paper", "why are you still on question number one?" As a teacher, I choose how and where to spend my time and energy. In this system, my time and energy could be spent encouraging working students with "hey, that's a great answer for number three", "fantastic, keep up the great effort", "nice, I like how you are working today." The whole vibe in my classroom became one of positivity. It was enjoyable to encourage those students that cared and wanted to learn, and from my experience the overwhelming majority of students cared. That doesn't mean I neglected the students that chose not to work. I continued to invite them into their learning. I also communicated with a parent or guardian if necessary to see if someone at home could encourage that student as well. ALL students matter, but how we approach those situations can make a tremendous difference. I saw it with a positive lens and encouraged ALL students. What I usually experienced was that all students eventually decided to work in my class without prompting.

2.) Now I have the time!

Every single year I hear the same struggle from teachers - "I just don't have enough time!" During the school year there are countless things to do including, but not limited to lesson plans, writing assessments, grading assessments, parent-teacher conferences, covering another teacher's class, professional development, school-wide meetings, learning new curriculum and software, emailing, and calling parents, and a "million" other little things that can overwhelm teachers. In my system, removing the daily pile of papers for grading frees up a teacher for so many other things. I think teachers start out each year with a clean slate and they think "OK, this is the year when I am going to be Superman or Wonder Woman! I'm going to do it all, amazing lesson plans, monitor and adjust throughout my lessons, collect all assignments, provide timely feedback, create meaningful assessments, implement the new curriculum, keep up to date with grades, stay in contact with families, attend the school events, coach athletic teams, run clubs, volunteer at the PTSO events!" (...and on and on and on). By October, the piles of papers have stacked up and the pressure of grading, meeting deadlines, and the rest has created so much tension and stress that the teacher feels like giving up knowing that the pace and expectations are unsustainable. He or she ends up saying, "If I only had more time!"

A great saying is "work smarter, not harder." In my system, eliminating the daily grading relieves such a huge burden and creates that much needed extra time. Now the teacher can do the three main things he or she was hired to do – create engaging lessons, teach those lessons, and accurately assess student learning. Furthermore, a teacher may find time to call families with good news about a student, attend school functions, coach a sport, sponsor a club, or contribute in other meaningful ways throughout the year without the risk of burning out. Teachers focused on teaching and assessing student learning. ***Teaching made simple, effective, and enjoyable to be sure!***

In this "stop grading papers" system, I guarantee your daily focus, stress level, enjoyment, effectiveness, and overall job satisfaction are going to improve. So, in the spirit of John Lennon - Imagine all the teachers not grading daily assignments but focusing on creating amazing lessons and assessing student learning. It's easy if you try.

Ch. 11 – Miscellaneous Q & A

As you continue in this profession, you will start to realize the practical, day-to-day details that make a difference. As I wrote at the beginning of this book, you do not have to be someone you are not, therefore the procedures and rules you deem necessary may not match the teacher across the hallway (or the ones I've written in this book). That's OK. That's the beauty of this profession. Your classroom and your style become your own.

In this chapter I am going to address some overarching questions for you to consider. This is not an exhaustive Q & A. You will have other considerations as you continue in your career. Each year you can keep the same procedures while adding new ones, or you can change procedures to better meet your students' needs. It's all about keeping things simple while still being productive and efficient. This leads to improved student performance, which is always the goal.

Q: What if a student does not respond when I ask him or her a question?

If, by chance, a student does not respond to a question you pose, you have a few options. I'll write about three for you to consider. The key is to try to not let students "off the hook."

Option 1 - Ask another student but come back to the first student.

Teacher: "What is the quiet signal we will use in this class? (Wait time of five seconds) Paul?"

Paul: "I don't know."

Teacher: "Paul, I'm going to ask another student, but then I am going to return to you so that you have an opportunity to explain to me. Andrea, will you explain the quiet signal please." (Choose someone that you are very confident will answer correctly).

Andrea: "You say eyes and ears in three, two, one and we get quiet, put our pencil down, raise our hand and turn to face you."

Teacher: "Excellent Andrea, thank you. Paul, can you explain the quiet signal, please?"

Paul: "You say eyes and ears in three, two, one. We get quiet, put our pen or pencil down, raise our hand, and turn and face you."

Teacher: "Fantastic. Thank you both for being attentive. That is an important quality that will help you be successful in this class."

Option 2 - Give that student 50/50

Teacher: "What is the quiet signal we will use in this class?" (Wait time of five seconds) "Paul?"

Paul: (shrugs)

Teacher: "Will I say, 'I need everyone's attention and then clap twice' or will I say, 'Eyes and ears on me in three, two, one'"?

Paul: "Eyes and ears on me in three, two, one."

Option 3 – provide a prompt

Teacher: "Class be prepared to tell me how many chambers are in the human heart (wait time of five seconds). Anthony?"

Anthony: "Uhhhh...I don't remember."

Teacher: "We talked yesterday that the structure of the heart includes atria and ventricles and that there are an equal number of those. Do you remember that?"

Anthony: "Yes, there were two atria and two ventricles so I think there must be four chambers."

Teacher: "Yes, correct! Excellent, Anthony."

If you try one of these and a student still sits quietly, don't force the issue. I wrote that we don't want to let students "off the hook", but we don't want to push it to a point where we've created a standoff. If a student sits and refuses to participate, a private side conversation or even a phone call home to encourage that student might be necessary. The bottom line is we cannot control our students or force them to answer questions. We can, however, encourage them to take risks and do their best. As I've written earlier, engaging in "micro-conversations" and picturing students wearing that sign that reads "Make me feel important" went a long way towards student participation in my classroom.

Q: What about the syllabus - when should I introduce students to it?

A: At some point in the first week, you can discuss your syllabus. Typically, the syllabus contains the curriculum broken down into units, supplies the student needs, the class rules and procedures and other considerations for students to keep in mind. Don't forget to include the fact that you will not be collecting work, but you will be giving weekly or bi-weekly assessments throughout the year.

I provided a syllabus every year but waited until day two to share it with students. Discussing the rules and procedures in the syllabus is important but think about it - you already had students practice a few procedures on the first day which is more effective than merely talking about them. Remember, students learn best by doing and not by being talked to. The syllabus is a necessary document, but you can wait until day two or three to discuss it with your students. Additionally, students should take it home to be signed by a parent or guardian acknowledging the fact that they have read and understood it.

I firmly believe that starting the year the way I suggested in the first few chapters is a much better use of the first day. Besides, most teachers start day one reading a syllabus line by line to their students. For a high school student, that might mean listening to a teacher talk about the syllabus six times in six different classes. You can be the teacher that starts differently, but still in a productive manner. Maybe that will spark the students' interest starting day one.

Q: What about other procedures besides the quiet signal, passing papers, and writing a heading?

A: Think about procedures that will make a difference and then teach the students by having them practice. The age and stage of your students will matter. For example, if you are teaching third grade, then an important procedure is how to line up and transition in the hallway. This means you should have students practice this procedure by doing it (possibly multiple times). If you are teaching high school, then this might not be a procedure you need to consider. Again, think of your classroom and think of the top five procedures that you think are the most critical for creating a productive and efficient classroom environment. The three I wrote about earlier were a quiet signal, passing papers in, and writing a heading. I would strongly suggest those be three that you practice on day one. How to walk to the pencil sharpener, sharpen a pencil, and walk back to sit down is a procedure you might want to teach (you'd be surprised at how one student sharpening a pencil can lead to off task behavior, especially for younger students). Whatever procedures you decide to incorporate into your classroom, begin practicing them as soon as possible so that ALL students have a clear understanding of how to implement them.

Q: What are some other classroom considerations?

A: There are two things that inevitably come up every year:

Q1.) What should a student do when he or she is absent?

I had a corkboard with MON – TUES – WED – THURS – FRI across the top. Any papers that were distributed for that day were pinned to the corkboard under the appropriate day. When a student had returned from being absent, he was taught to check the corkboard and grab any papers he had missed. In addition to grabbing any papers they missed, returning students were also instructed to first check with their shoulder partner to get some insight about those papers. Often that was enough to help the student, but if they were still unsure, the student was instructed to come to me at an appropriate time so I could give a detailed explanation of what was expected. I informed students that they should wait until I could give them my undivided attention to help them understand any missing work that they had.

What you want to avoid is a student coming to you on, say, a Wednesday at the beginning of class and asking, "I was absent Monday and Tuesday - what did I miss?" Remember, your time and energy each day are limited. You don't want to waste either by digging out the papers the absent student missed, and you certainly don't have time to explain those papers in the first few minutes of class. Keep in mind the rest of the students are doing the warm-up and it is critical that you keep those students on time. So again, teach students to get any missing papers from your corkboard and to talk to their partner (Remember, you numbered them "ones" and "twos", so each student has a partner). Often that is enough to catch them up, but if they still need support, a student that was absent can come to you at the appropriate time for an explanation.

Q2.) What does a student do when he or she needs to use the restroom?

Depending upon the age and maturity of your students you can decide what the most appropriate procedure for restroom use is. I taught high school for nineteen years so my perspective may be slightly different than yours, however there are probably enough similarities regardless of what grade you are teaching. I had students raise their hand and ask permission. Usually I said yes right away, however occasionally I felt it was important for all students to be in the room in which case I would respond "Can you wait about 10 minutes?" Usually students could wait, however if they couldn't I did not hold them back. (Sidenote: When a female student asked to see the nurse I automatically responded yes). Create a system in which students sign out when leaving and sign back in when they return. Most schools have the expectation that students take a bathroom pass so I would suggest hanging your pass near the door or sticking it in your corkboard. I would also suggest laminating the pass so it can be used throughout the entire year. Using the restroom is a natural, everyday part of school so you should clearly explain to students the procedure for signing out and the expectation for returning in a timely manner.

Q: What about rules?

I emphasized to my students that rules are really expectations to help create a positive and productive culture and I used the example of flying on an airplane to reinforce that. I started by asking my students if any of them had ever flown on an airplane. Usually at least a few had, which made this example really sink it. After asking, I went on to explain that people get on the plane in an orderly fashion. Typically, by letter and number. For example, people with a boarding pass of A 1-15 get on first, then people with A 16-30, B1-15, etc. This continues until the last group is called to board the plane. I asked students to tell me why they think this system is in place. Usually, students said exactly what I was hoping they would. The rules for getting on a plane are for the safety of the passengers and for the efficiency of the airline. Airlines earn a better reputation and consequently make more money based on being on time. The more orderly and efficiently passengers get on a plane the better the chance the flight will take off and land on time. Once I gave that analogy, I related that to our classroom and I emphasized that just like an airline has rules for safety and efficiency, our classroom needs rules for the same reasons.

Your rules should be posted in the classroom on a piece of butcher paper or a poster. My suggestion is no more than five rules written in a positive way (e.g., "Speak kindly to others") not in a negative way (e.g., "Don't be rude"). The rules for your classroom might not match every other teacher's rules. That's okay. For example, you may not want students to get up without permission so make that a rule in your classroom and write it in a positive way on your butcher paper. ("Please ask permission to get up for any reason"). Think of the top five rules that will contribute to a productive classroom environment for you and your students, list them in a positive way, and then post them on the wall for everyone to see. My rules were typically as follows:

1. Keep your work area clean.

2. Be in your seat when the bell rings to begin class.

3. Have all your materials out and ready to use when the bell rings to begin class.

4. Please ask permission to get up for any reason.

5. Speak kindly to others and use appropriate language.

Q: What if I don't think of something until a few weeks into the year?

A: It's OK! You can practice the procedures that will help your classroom run efficiently and productively, and you can discuss your rules and make sure that students know what to do when they are absent or need to use the restroom. You can do all of this but realize a week or two into the year that the students would benefit from the addition of another procedure. It's OK to add things as you need to. There is no law that says you cannot add or modify procedures as the year goes on. What you want to avoid though is changing things unnecessarily or too often. Like I wrote earlier, students like routine and structure so do your best to create a classroom that has both and stick with it.

Q: Can I share my enthusiasm for my content with my students during the first week?

A: Absolutely! While it is critical to teach procedures and establish routines on day one and beyond, there is nothing wrong with giving students a "sneak preview" of some of the more interesting topics of your class. Very early in the year, my students did an inquiry lab in which they tried to determine why water seemingly defies gravity and moves up a glass jar. This lab never failed to get students excited and pique their interest in my class. Obviously, I would encourage you to start your year using the strategies I've written in this book, but there is nothing wrong with showing your students your passion for your subject early and often or doing an activity that will get them excited to take the course.

Q: What if some, most, or all students meet the lesson objective with time to spare?

A: I had another piece of butcher paper on my wall titled, "I'm finished, now what?" Under the title I wrote several options for students including:

- Grab a magazine and read an article.
- Clean and organize your backpack.
- Write a letter of gratitude to someone you know.
- Sit quietly and relax.
- Do work for another class.

You can include these and any other additional options that will keep kids productive and allow them to use their time wisely without becoming disruptive.

Chapter 12 – Closing thoughts

<u>What an incredible opportunity!</u> Education is a powerful difference maker in the life of a child. As your students' teacher, you have a chance to make all children realize their potential, help students recognize their strengths, and help them understand how to make the most of those strengths. You will also help students understand and overcome areas where they struggle. Sometimes teaching a child to persevere is every bit as important as teaching them how to write a catchy introductory paragraph or analyze the parts of a cell. You can shape a child's hopes and dreams. Most importantly, you can give them the confidence and belief to help them move towards whatever it is that they aspire to. Let's be honest – EVERYONE wants a great teacher for their child, but not everyone is willing to become that great teacher. You have chosen to become that great teacher! You have an opportunity to make such a positive impact on your students, not just when they are your students, but beyond. Your influence is limitless. I hope you see how awesome your opportunity can be! For those of you that are new to the profession - welcome! You will soon understand the allure of teaching. For those of you that are not new to the profession, you are probably nodding right now thinking 'Yep, there's just something about this profession that keeps me in it.' It's not "having my summer off", but something else. Something less tangible. You'll know it when you're in it and unless you're in it, it's hard to understand. Rest assured that you have chosen a career that will give you some of the most meaningful moments of your life. Remember how I started this book, ***I want your first day to be productive and enjoyable, but I want your last day, and every day in between, to be the same.***

Sound impossible? I'm here to tell you it's NOT.

Now that you have completed this book, my hope is you believe you can make it happen. I wish you the best moving forward, and I hope that teaching becomes the career that helps you inspire your students and always brings you joy and satisfaction.

Afterword: When I started this book, technology in the classroom was not as prominent as it is now. Some of the strategies I write about involve paper-based activities versus doing things on a tablet or computer. I am confident that shouldn't change the importance of any of the ideas in this book. As an example, the day one quiz can still be given on a computer-based program rather than using paper and pencil. The other ideas I write about like procedures, lesson plan design, engaging in micro-conversations, and other suggestions and tips are still relevant whether technology is the mode of learning, a more traditional paper-based approach is used, or a combination of the two.